# beautiful MERCY

## EXPERIENCING GOD'S UNCONDITIONAL LOVE SO WE CAN SHARE IT WITH OTHERS

DynamicCatholic.com
Be Bold. Be Catholic.®

Published by Beacon Publishing.

ISBN (Hardcover): 978-1-942611-50-9
ISBN (Softcover): 978-1-942611-57-8



For more information on bulk copies of this title or other books and CDs available through the Dynamic Catholic Book Program, please visit www.DynamicCatholic.com or call 859-980-7900.

The Dynamic Catholic Institute
5081 Olympic Blvd • Erlanger • Kentucky • 41018
Phone: 1-859-980-7900
Email: info@DynamicCatholic.com

Design by Jenny Miller

Printed in the United States of America

# TABLE OF CONTENTS

# PRELUDE: WE ALL NEED A LITTLE MERCY

*MATTHEW KELLY*

Adam struggles to get out of bed each morning. It isn't until he completes his daily stretches that his right leg will loosen up enough for him to walk. He is just twenty-six years old, but his leg functions like that of a man much older.

It's been two years to the day since Adam was honorably discharged from the Marines. Injured in a firefight, he will always walk with a limp. He smiles, though, as he thinks about the day ahead. His parents are throwing a party to commemorate his return home. His whole family will be there.

He finishes his stretches and rests in a chair by the window. He pauses, takes a deep breath, and begins to pray. He thanks God for his wife and asks him to guide her in her day. He prays for his family and friends, each by name. He prays for all the men and women still in active duty. He prays for the conversion of his enemies. Finally he offers the pain he will feel in his leg for all the men and women he fought alongside who do not get to celebrate a return home the way he does.

He prays for their souls, that they may rest eternally in the peace of God.

Adam winces as he rises and grabs for the cane by the bed. He joins his wife for breakfast and they begin the day together.

That's beautiful mercy.

---

Every morning David wakes up at six thirty. Every morning, that is, except Friday. On Fridays he gets up at four o'clock. He shaves, showers, and dresses for work. At five o'clock he kisses his wife and checks on his kids before leaving for the day. As he looks at them sleeping in their beds, he smiles and says a quick prayer thanking God for his family.

On Fridays David serves the breadline in the city where he works. He puts on a smock, gloves, and a hairnet to serve those who do not have the means to provide for themselves. On any given Friday David can be seen serving the homeless, the working poor, addicts, and the mentally ill. Some say thank you, others thank God for him, and still others don't say a word, often returning his smile with a scowl.

Every Friday he looks forward to seeing the regulars, Jeff and Alex. After serving food for close to an hour, David is able to sit with them and share a cup of coffee. The trio shares stories about their kids and favorite athletes growing up. All three enjoy the company far more than the coffee.

David isn't a morning person and doesn't enjoy the four a.m. wake-up call. He struggles to choke down the stale coffee and if he had a choice, he would never wear a hairnet.

But every Friday, as sure as the sun will rise, he can be found serving the breadline.

That's beautiful mercy.

---

Catherine and Howard have worked hard for everything they own in life; money doesn't come easily. They've done their best to raise their four children. They've sacrificed family vacations and dreams of a second car for baseball gloves, ice skates, books for school, etc.

The most challenging times came when Howard was periodically laid off from his job. He never hesitated to take whatever job was available so that his kids wouldn't have to suffer. In fact, they'll never know that there was a time when he worked as a garbage collector to ensure food was on the table.

Catherine makes curtains and sews clothing. Howard fixes cars and has mastered the house's plumbing system. They've counted pennies and made ends meet, never asking for anything in return.

One day, their youngest daughter, Samantha, comes home from school with news. The night prior, her best friend, Tanya, was thrown out of her house. Tanya's mother chose her new boyfriend over her daughter. Tanya is eighteen, alone, and on the streets, without a penny to her name.

Without hesitation, Catherine and Howard welcome Tanya into their home. They open their doors for her, will provide for her, and will find a way to make it work for their family.

That's beautiful mercy.

Mary Anne fell ill with pneumonia at the age of eighty-seven. She survived but the recovery has left her bedridden. She is weak, no longer able to carry out the daily demands of feeding, washing, and dressing herself. She has gone from being an incredibly active and self-sufficient woman to depending completely on those around her.

Mary Anne has struggled with this transition in her life. Her self-worth was wrapped up in her ability to give. "What's the purpose of living life stuck in a bed?" she would ask God. For the first time in her life, she has grappled with despair.

Nearly every day, despite an hour-long commute each way, Mary Anne's daughter bursts in the door with a huge smile and a story to tell. Danielle has her mother's energy and joy for life. Mary Anne's despair has met its match in Danielle. Together they laugh and talk through the hard reality of Mary Anne's new life. Danielle helps keep some semblance of normalcy for her mother by dyeing her hair to cover the gray and painting her nails so she has something pretty to look at when the nights get lonely.

When asked by her husband why she feels the need to visit her mother so often Danielle responds by saying, simply, "As a kid I went to bed every night knowing I was loved because of my mother. She deserves to feel the same way now."

That's beautiful mercy.

---

Serving others is at the core of the mission God has for his children. When it comes to serving people in need, our family, the Catholic Church, has an incredible track record. The Church feeds more people, houses more people, clothes more people, educates more people, and takes care of more sick people than any other institution in the world. And the Church achieves this through the action of ordinary Catholics like you and me.

For thousands of years God has been using ordinary people to do extraordinary things. He delights in dynamic collaboration with humanity. He doesn't necessarily choose the people who are the best educated or who are good-looking; he doesn't choose people because they are in positions of power and authority; he doesn't always choose the most eloquent and persuasive. There is only one type of person God has used powerfully throughout history: He does incredible things with the people who make themselves available to him; it is the prerequisite for mission.

Pope Francis has called for an extraordinary Year of Mercy. He is inviting each of us to spend the next year with mercy as a focal point of our spirituality. This is a tremendous opportunity to make yourself available to God.

Before I became a father, I thought I knew something about the love God the Father has for me. Then my son Walter was born. I found myself constantly yearning to be with him. He couldn't walk or talk. All he did was eat, and sleep, and need his diaper changed. But I loved being with him.

Over the years, that hasn't changed. As my wife and I have had more children, I yearn to be with each of them in the same way. I love my children so much it's crazy, really. And before I had them I just didn't understand. But as I began to think about this great love I have for my children, the love of God took on a whole new meaning. Because if I can love my children as much as I do, and I am broken and wounded and flawed and limited, imagine how much God loves us. This thought was overwhelming to me and took my relationship with God to the next level.

The same goes for God's mercy. We may think we know that he loves us or that his mercy is boundless, but have we experienced it? Have we been the hands and feet of God, the living embodiment of his mercy to those around us?

I think Pope Francis has called for this Year of Mercy because he wants us to connect on a personal level with God's mercy. But how do we do it? Fortunately for us, there is genius in Catholicism. The Church has given us the works of mercy to help bring the love of God to other people. How beautiful is that?

The works of mercy are broken up into two categories: the corporal works of mercy and the spiritual works of mercy.

The corporal works of mercy are concerned with meeting the physical needs of others. They are:

- feed the hungry
- give drink to the thirsty
- clothe the naked
- shelter the homeless
- visit the sick
- visit the imprisoned
- bury the dead

The spiritual works of mercy, on the other hand, are designed to meet the spiritual needs of others. They are:

- instruct the ignorant
- counsel the doubtful
- correct sinners

- bear wrongs patiently
- forgive offenses willingly
- comfort the afflicted
- pray for the living and the dead

It's simple, but imagine how the world would be different if everyone practiced just one work of mercy each day. How would the world be different if these works of mercy defined the way we live our lives? There is genius in Catholicism, but sadly it is little known and practiced. At Dynamic Catholic we are committed to giving you simple and practical ways to live out the genius of Catholicism and become the-best-version-of-yourself.

For this book, we've enlisted the help of some incredible authors in the Church. These authors have taken the fourteen works of spiritual and corporal mercy and provided simple, practical ways for you to understand them better and to incorporate them into your everyday life.

I hope you pray through this book and invite the mercy of God to transform your life, because in the end it's all about God's mercy.

Sometimes the best way to think about life is to reflect upon death. When I think about my life and how I have offended God, all the opportunities I have had to love that I have turned my back on, how little I have done with the gifts he has given me, I hope he is merciful. When I reflect upon all my faults and failings, my mistakes and sins, my pride and arrogance, I hope he is merciful.

I believe he is.

In the end we each must fall at the feet of God and beg for mercy. In the end it all comes down to mercy. Let us now strive to show others the mercy we hope to receive.

---

Matthew Kelly is the *New York Times* bestselling author of *The Rhythm of Life* and twenty other books, including *Rediscover Jesus.*

# INTRODUCTION: AN INVITATION TO MERCY

*POPE FRANCIS*

Jesus Christ is the face of the Father's mercy. These words might well sum up the mystery of the Christian faith. Mercy has become living and visible in Jesus of Nazareth, reaching its culmination in him. The Father, "rich in mercy" (Ephesians 2:4), after having revealed his name to Moses as "a God merciful and gracious, slow to anger, and abounding in steadfast love and faithfulness" (Exodus 34:6), has never ceased to show, in various ways throughout history, his divine nature. In the "fullness of time" (Galatians 4:4), when everything had been arranged according to his plan of salvation, he sent his only Son into the world, born of the Virgin Mary, to reveal his love for us in a definitive way. Whoever sees Jesus sees the Father (cf. John 14:9). Jesus of Nazareth, by his words, his actions, and his entire person reveals the mercy of God.

We need constantly to contemplate the mystery of mercy. It is a wellspring of joy, serenity, and peace. Our salvation depends on it. Mercy: the word reveals the very mystery of the Most Holy Trinity. Mercy: the ultimate and supreme act by which God comes to meet us. Mercy: the fundamental law that dwells in the heart of every person who looks sincerely into the eyes of his brothers and sisters on the path of life. Mercy: the bridge that connects God and man, opening our hearts to the hope of being loved forever despite our sinfulness.

At times we are called to gaze even more attentively on mercy so that we may become a more effective sign of the Father's action in our lives. For this reason I have proclaimed an *Extraordinary Jubilee of Mercy* as a special time for the Church, a time when the witness of believers might grow stronger and more effective.

The Holy Year will open on 8 December 2015, the Solemnity of the Immaculate Conception. This liturgical feast day recalls God's action from the very beginning of the history of mankind. After the sin of Adam and Eve, God did not wish to leave humanity alone in the throes of evil. And so he turned his gaze to Mary, holy and immaculate in love (cf. Ephesians 1:4), choosing her to be the Mother of man's Redeemer. When faced with the gravity of sin, God responds with the fullness of mercy. Mercy will always be greater than any sin, and no one can place limits on the love of God who is ever ready to forgive. I will have the joy of opening the Holy Door on the Solemnity of the Immaculate Conception. On that day, the Holy Door will become a *Door of Mercy* through which anyone who enters will experience the love of God who consoles, pardons, and instills hope.

---

With our eyes fixed on Jesus and his merciful gaze, we experience the love of the Most Holy Trinity. The mission Jesus received from the Father was that of revealing the mystery of divine love in its fullness. "God is love" (1 John 4:8,16), John affirms for the first and only time in all of Holy Scripture. This love has now been made visible and tangible in Jesus' entire life. His person is nothing but love, a love given gratuitously. The relationships he forms with the people who approach him manifest something entirely unique and unrepeatable. The signs he works, especially in favor of sinners, the poor, the marginalized, the sick, and the suffering, are all meant to teach mercy. Everything in him speaks of mercy. Nothing in him is devoid of compassion.

Jesus, seeing the crowds of people who followed him, realized that they were tired and exhausted, lost and without a guide, and he felt deep compassion for them (cf. Matthew 9:36). On the basis of this compassionate love he healed the sick who were presented to him (cf. Matthew 14:14), and with just a few loaves of bread and fish he satisfied the enormous crowd (cf. Matthew 15:37). What moved Jesus in all of these situations was nothing other than mercy, with which he read the hearts of those he encountered and responded to their deepest need. When he came upon the widow of Nain taking her son out for burial, he felt great compassion for the immense suffering of this grieving mother, and he gave back her son by raising him from the dead (cf. Luke 7:15). After freeing the demoniac in the country of the Gerasenes, Jesus entrusted him with this mission: "Go home to your friends, and tell them how much the Lord has done for you, and how he has had mercy on you" (Mark 5:19). The calling of Matthew is also presented within the context of mercy.

Passing by the tax collector's booth, Jesus looked intently at Matthew. It was a look full of mercy that forgave the sins of that man, a sinner and a tax collector, whom Jesus chose—against the hesitation of the disciples—to become one of the Twelve. Saint Bede the Venerable, commenting on this Gospel passage, wrote that Jesus looked upon Matthew with merciful love and chose him: *miserando atque eligendo*. This expression impressed me so much that I chose it for my episcopal motto.

In the parables devoted to mercy, Jesus reveals the nature of God as that of a Father who never gives up until he has forgiven the wrong and overcome rejection with compassion and mercy. We know these parables well, three in particular: the lost sheep, the lost coin, and the father with two sons (cf. Luke 15:1–32). In these parables, God is always presented as full of joy, especially when he pardons. In them we find the core of the Gospel and of our faith, because mercy is presented as a force that overcomes everything, filling the heart with love and bringing consolation through pardon.

From another parable, we cull an important teaching for our Christian lives. In reply to Peter's question about how many times it is necessary to forgive, Jesus says: "I do not say seven times, but seventy times seven times" (Matthew 18:22). He then goes on to tell the parable of the "ruthless servant," who, called by his master to return a huge amount, begs him on his knees for mercy. His master cancels his debt. But he then meets a fellow servant who owes him a few cents and who in turn begs on his knees for mercy, but the first servant refuses his request and throws him into jail. When the master hears of the matter, he becomes infuriated and, summoning the first servant back to him, says, "Should not you have had mercy on your fellow servant, as I had mercy on you?" (Matthew 18:33). Jesus concludes, "So also my heavenly Father will do to every one of you, if you do not forgive your brother from your heart" (Matthew 18:35).

This parable contains a profound teaching for all of us. Jesus affirms that mercy is not only an action of the Father, it becomes a criterion for ascertaining who his true children are. In short, we are called to show mercy because mercy has first been shown to us. Pardoning offences becomes the clearest expression of merciful love, and for us Christians it is an imperative from which we cannot excuse ourselves. At times how hard it seems to forgive! And yet pardon is the instrument placed into our fragile hands to attain serenity of heart. To let go of anger, wrath, violence, and revenge are necessary conditions to living joyfully. Let us therefore heed the Apostle's exhortation: "Do not let the sun go down on your anger" (Ephesians 4:26). Above all, let us listen to the words of Jesus who made mercy an ideal of life and a criterion for the credibility of our faith: "Blessed are the merciful, for they shall obtain mercy" (Matthew 5:7): the beatitude to which we should particularly aspire in this Holy Year.

As we can see in Sacred Scripture, mercy is a key word that indicates God's action towards us. He does not limit himself merely to affirming his love, but makes it visible and tangible. Love, after all, can never be just an abstraction. By its very nature, it indicates something concrete: intentions, attitudes, and behaviors that are shown in daily living. The mercy of God is his loving concern for each one of us. He feels responsible; that is, he desires our wellbeing and he wants to see us happy, full of joy, and peaceful. This is the path which the merciful love of Christians must also travel. As the Father loves, so do his children. Just as he is merciful, so we are called to be merciful to each other.

Mercy is the very foundation of the Church's life. All of her pastoral activity should be caught up in the tenderness she makes present to believers; nothing in her preaching and in her witness to the world can be lacking in mercy. The Church's very credibility is seen in how she shows merciful and compassionate love. The Church "has an endless desire to show mercy." Perhaps we have long since forgotten how to show and live the way of mercy. The temptation, on the one hand, to focus exclusively on justice made us forget that this is only the first, albeit necessary and indispensable step. But the Church needs to go beyond and strive for a higher and more important goal. On the other hand, sad to say, we must admit that the practice of mercy is waning in the wider culture. In some cases the word seems to have dropped out of use. However, without a witness to mercy, life becomes fruitless and sterile, as if sequestered in a barren desert. The time has come for the Church to take up the joyful call to mercy once more. It is time to return to the basics and to bear the weaknesses and struggles of our brothers and sisters. Mercy is the force that reawakens us to new life and instills in us the courage to look to the future with hope.

---

The Church is commissioned to announce the mercy of God, the beating heart of the Gospel, which in its own way must penetrate the heart and mind of every person. The Spouse of Christ must pattern her behavior after the Son of God who went out to everyone without exception. In the present day, as the Church is charged with the task of the new evangelization, the theme of mercy needs to be proposed again and again with new enthusiasm and renewed pastoral action. It is absolutely essential for the Church and for the credibility of her message that she herself live and testify to mercy. Her language and her gestures must transmit mercy, so as to touch the hearts of all people and inspire them once more to find the road that leads to the Father.

The Church's first truth is the love of Christ. The Church makes herself a servant of this love and mediates it to all people: a love that forgives and expresses itself in the gift of oneself. Consequently, wherever the Church is present, the mercy of the Father must be evident. In our parishes, communities, associations and movements, in a word, wherever there are Christians, everyone should find an oasis of mercy.

---

*Merciful like the Father*, therefore, is the "motto" of this Holy Year. In mercy, we find proof of how God loves us. He gives his entire self, always, freely, asking nothing in return. He comes to our aid whenever we call upon him. What a beautiful thing that the Church begins her daily prayer with the words, "O God, come to my assistance. O Lord, make haste to help me" (Psalm 70:2)! The assistance we ask for is already the first step of God's mercy toward us. He comes to assist us in our weakness. And his help consists in helping us accept his presence and closeness to us. Day after day, touched by his compassion, we also can become compassionate towards others.

---

It is my burning desire that, during this Jubilee, the Christian people may reflect on the *corporal and spiritual works of mercy*. It will be a way to reawaken our conscience, too often grown dull in the face of poverty. And let us enter more deeply into the heart of the Gospel where the poor have a special experience of God's mercy. Jesus introduces us to these works of mercy in his preaching so that we can know whether or not we are living as his disciples. Let us rediscover these *corporal works of mercy*: to feed the hungry, give drink to the thirsty, clothe the naked, welcome the stranger, heal the sick, visit the imprisoned, and bury the dead. And let us not forget the *spiritual works of mercy*: to counsel the doubtful, instruct the ignorant, admonish sinners, comfort the afflicted, forgive offenses, bear patiently those who do us ill, and pray for the living and the dead.

We cannot escape the Lord's words to us, and they will serve as the criteria upon which we will be judged: whether we have fed the hungry and given drink to the thirsty, welcomed the stranger and clothed the naked, or spent time with the sick and those in prison (cf. Matthew 25:31–45). Moreover, we will be asked if we have helped others to escape the doubt that causes them to fall into despair and which is often a source of loneliness; if we have helped to overcome the ignorance in which millions of people live, especially children deprived of the necessary means to free them from the bonds of poverty; if we have been close to the lonely and afflicted; if we have forgiven those who have offended us and have rejected all forms of anger and hate that lead to violence; if we have had the kind of patience God shows, who is so patient with us; and if we have commended our brothers and sisters to the Lord in prayer. In each of these "little ones," Christ himself is present. His flesh becomes visible in the flesh of the tortured, the crushed, the scourged, the malnourished, and the exiled... to be acknowledged, touched, and cared for by us. Let us not forget the words of Saint John of the Cross: "as we prepare to leave this life, we will be judged on the basis of love."

---

I present, therefore, this Extraordinary Jubilee Year dedicated to living out in our daily lives the mercy which the Father constantly extends to all of us. In this Jubilee Year, let us allow God to surprise us. He never tires of casting open the doors of his heart and of repeating that he loves us and wants to share his love with us. The Church feels the urgent need to proclaim God's mercy. Her life is authentic and credible only when she becomes a convincing herald of mercy. She knows that her primary task, especially at a moment full of great hopes and signs of contradiction, is to introduce everyone to the great mystery of God's mercy by contemplating the face of Christ. The Church is called above all to be a credible witness to mercy, professing it and living it as the core of the revelation of Jesus Christ. From the heart of the Trinity, from the depths of the mystery of God, the great river of mercy wells up and overflows unceasingly. It is a spring that will never run dry, no matter how many people draw from it. Every time someone is in need, he or she can approach it, because the mercy of God never ends. The profundity of the mystery surrounding it is as inexhaustible as the richness which springs up from it.

In this Jubilee Year, may the Church echo the word of God that resounds strong and clear as a message and a sign of pardon, strength, aid, and love. May she never tire of extending mercy, and be ever patient in offering compassion and comfort. May the Church become the voice of every man and woman, and repeat confidently without end: “Be mindful of your mercy, O Lord, and your steadfast love, for they have been from of old” (Psalm 25:6).

PART ONE

# THE CORPORAL WORKS OF MERCY

*"Do not neglect to show hospitality to strangers, for thereby some have entertained angels unawares."*

*HEBREWS 13:2*

# 1

# HARBOR THE HOMELESS

**HOME. IT PLAYS AN IMPORTANT** part in our lives. Have you ever wondered where you were going to sleep at night? There are nearly 100 million people in the world who have to ask that question every day.

# WELCOMING MERCY

*CARDINAL DONALD WUERL*

The well-known story of the Little Sisters of the Poor begins in 1839 when Jeanne Jugan, on a cold winter day, made the decision to bring in from the bitter weather an elderly, blind, infirm widow. As the story is related, the poor woman at this point in her life had no one to care for her and was in fact without a home. For more than 175 years since, the Little Sisters of the Poor, with their homes in more than thirty countries, have been opening their doors to people who might otherwise not have a home.

Homelessness today takes on many diverse forms, and how we respond to the corporal work of mercy to house the homeless must be equally creative. Jeanne Jugan, canonized by Pope Benedict XVI on October 11, 2009, could not have carried out her work of mercy without the assistance of others capable of providing the necessary support, including the actual "home."

Often when I make requests on behalf of Catholic Charities or other archdiocesan social service providers, I remind the faithful that while each one of us, individually, cannot always be there to respond to every person in need, and many times we simply do not have the personal resources to be able to meet that need, nonetheless we are still capable of being part of the answer. Nowhere is this truer than when we reply to the call to house the homeless.

Rarely and with few exceptions are we able to actually open the doors of our own homes and bring in the homeless. But we are able to see to it that they do have a "home." We can also see to it that they receive many of the human amenities that we associate with our own homes.

When looking for a place to live, we may think in terms of "room and board"—a roof over our heads and regular meals. Providing a home for the homeless involves those elements. All over this country and certainly within the dioceses that I have been privileged to serve, there are shelters for the homeless staffed and operated by Catholic Charities or other Catholic social service providers. This happens only because there are many people who are willing to contribute those services that make possible the care in each facility.

Another example of housing the homeless is the countless "homes" run by Catholic housing services that provide modest yet dignified apartments, which would otherwise be beyond the grasp of people of greatly restricted means living on fixed minimum incomes.

But we also need to speak about the meals we associate with home. Once again my mind's eye turns to those soup kitchens, meal vans, and parish food pantries that provide a meal for those in need.

A couple of years ago, in the Archdiocese of Washington, we came to realize that the many, many homeless who spend a night in a shelter are by law required to leave the shelter early each morning. They do so with empty pockets and empty stomachs. This led to a program called "A Cup of Joe." As they leave, the homeless now can receive, through Catholic Charities, a brown bag containing what for them has become their regular breakfast. These are handed out by the thousands. And they are prepared by hundreds of volunteers young and old, including youngsters from our elementary and secondary schools, who now vie with one another to help the homeless.

In *The Merchant of Venice*, William Shakespeare writes, "The quality of mercy is not strain'd . . . is twice bless'd: it blesseth him who gives and him that takes." How true it is! While we cannot always be present to meet every need of every homeless person or see that at any given moment they find room and board—a roof and meals—we can be a blessing to them and meet our own obligations toward them. While personally I cannot always be there, our institutions, our homes, our shelters, and Catholic Charities are all present all the time.

Not that long ago while in Rome for meetings, I walked along the colonnades to the right of the great facade of the Basilica of Saint Peter to find the newly installed showers for the poor. More recently I learned of the new shelter for the homeless going up on the via dei Penitenzieri, just a stone's throw from the same square. Clearly the successor to Peter, Bishop of Rome, Pope Francis is in fact giving all of us an example of how today we can house the homeless.

There is yet another form of housing the homeless. This may touch a little closer to our own home. In John's Gospel, as Jesus hangs on the cross, his concern now turns to his mother and what will become of her. Then he says to St. John, "Behold your mother." The Gospel tells us, "And from that hour, the disciple took her to his own home" (John 19:27). Sometimes the call to house the homeless brings with it the challenge of our own family members who may no longer be capable of that independence that has so marked their lives. In this time when we not only celebrate a Year of Mercy, but conclude two Synods of Bishops on the Family, we are reminded that our love and mercy must always begin at home. Family must always be home, the shelter for the lonely, disabled, or elderly family members who can no longer care for themselves. Family members should never feel homeless, no matter what their condition.

As Shakespeare pointed out, mercy is a two-way street. It is not something we do *to* others; it is a way in which we share together *with* others the human condition so that words such as *brother* and *sister* are not simply a manner of speaking but a manner of living.

---

Cardinal Donald Wuerl is the Archbishop of Washington and the bestselling author of many books, including *The Catholic Way*.

*"He who has a bountiful eye will be blessed,*
*for he shares his bread with the poor."*

*PROVERBS 22:9*

2

# FEED THE HUNGRY

**WHEN WAS THE LAST TIME** you were hungry—truly hungry? Three million children die of under nutrition worldwide every year. That's one child every four seconds. Think about that the next time you use the words "I'm starving" to describe your hunger.

# GENEROUS MERCY

*FR. LARRY RICHARDS*

We must feed the hungry or be damned! Did I get your attention? I hope so! The very core of Christianity is not the focus on self but the forgetfulness of self and the focus on others. Jesus tells us: "This is how all people will know that you are My disciples, that you love one another" (John 13:35, NAB). The spiritual and corporal works of mercy are love put into action. Too many people focus on just the spiritual works of mercy, which are important, but we also must live the corporal works, which focus on the physical needs of others. As we read in James' Epistle: "If a brother or sister has . . . no food for the day, and one of you says to them, 'Go in peace, keep warm and eat well,' but you do not give them the necessities of the body, what good is it?" (James 2:15–16, NAB). The work of mercy that we need to reflect on is the traditional first corporal work of mercy, which is to "feed the hungry."

To feed the hungry is *not* an option for the Christian. Some Christians may say, "If I have the chance, then I might get around to doing it." But how far from the truth that is! Jesus makes it very clear that we *must* take care of others if we hope to get to heaven. Now, this is not being saved by works, but putting into practice the grace that has been given to us; what we believe as Christians is that our God loved us so much that he became one of us to save us. He calls us to be people who love like he does, that we love others to save them as he did. He fed the five thousand because they were hungry.

I used to teach all boys at a Catholic high school, and I would give the kids the questions and answers for every test, and yet I still failed an average of eight students a year! Even when we know the answers, some people will not prepare themselves. Jesus gives us the questions and answers for how we will be judged in the Judgment of the Nations, in Matthew 25:31–46 (NAB). In verses 41 and 42 he makes it very clear: "Then He will say to those on His left, 'Depart from Me, you accursed, into the eternal fire prepared for the devil and His angels. For I was hungry and you gave Me no food.'" In the end, the sins of omission will be the greatest sins.

What will you do on Judgment Day when you stand before God and he asks you: Why in your lifetime did an average of twenty thousand children in the world die every day because of hunger-related causes? Will you say, "I am not sure, God, but they were not my kids," to which he will respond, "No, they were mine"? The point is that we need to make sure we live what we believe and that we prepare ourselves for the final judgment. We should not do any of this out of fear or guilt, but out of mercy and love!

Almost everyone I have ever met desires mercy, but if you want mercy, you need to *give* mercy. I often wonder what would happen if I were the one who needed food. Or what if a member of my family needed food? I would do everything in my power to have that need fulfilled. The people who need to be fed are our brothers and sisters and God's sons and daughters, and whatever we do or fail to do for them, we do or fail to do for Jesus.

So what does "feed the hungry" look like practically? Well, we can begin by deciding to start giving money on a monthly basis to support one of the organizations that take care of feeding the poor. You can adopt a child in a poor country. You can give money to a food bank. You can volunteer at a food pantry or an organization that feeds people. You can make sandwiches and take them to the homeless. You can give money to homeless shelters. You can carry change in your pocket, and every time you meet a beggar, you give him or her something, even if it is just a quarter. You can take food to a neighbor who is shut in and does not often get a home-cooked meal. There are many things that you can do; you just have to do it.

We began with "We must feed the hungry or be damned," and now you might be thinking: "OK, OK, I should start to do something." But thoughts and good intentions are not enough—you need to turn these thoughts into reality. So what are *you* going to do? God wants to use *you* for his glory. He wants to use *you* to reach out and feed others. He wants *you* to be the person of mercy and to be his instrument for the hungry. Let God use *you* and start to change the world! When you do this, then you can be the one who hears Jesus say: "Come, you are blessed by My Father. Inherit the kingdom prepared for *you* from the foundation of the world. For I was hungry and *you* gave Me food . . ." (Matthew 25:34–35, NAB).

---

Fr. Larry Richards hosts the EWTN radio show, *The Reason for Our Hope*, and is the author of *Be a Man! Becoming the Man God Created You to Be* and *Surrender! The Life-Changing Power of Doing God's Will.*

# ACTIVE MERCY

*FR. MICHAEL GAITLEY, MIC*

There are many ways to satisfy the hunger of our neighbor. Most cities and towns have soup kitchens and food pantries that welcome volunteers. (A soup kitchen provides meals for the poor and homeless. A food pantry collects donated food, such as through a can drive, to help families and individuals who live near the poverty line.) Volunteering from time to time or even regularly at a soup kitchen, organizing a food drive, and helping to start a food pantry at your parish are all effective ways of feeding the hungry.

Here's another suggestion: Make dinner for a family in need. One of the things my sister most appreciates is when neighbors and friends made dinner for her family while she was in the hospital—usually after delivering one of her babies. Every one of us has probably gone through a trial when we were so sick, suffering, or stressed out that we weren't able to prepare a meal for ourselves, let alone for anyone else. Making a meal for someone or for a family in such a situation is a great work of mercy. As my sister says, "The greatest thing you can do for a mom is to make a meal for her family!" She was kind of joking, but not really. It is a great thing.

This gets me thinking that homemakers, like my sister, who cook for their families are themselves putting mercy into action by giving food to the hungry and drink to the thirsty. They may not realize they're doing a work of mercy, but they are, and it's important that they recognize it. So many of our actions can be transformed from what seems like meaningless labor into works of love—*if we consciously choose to make them so*. In other words, every day, each one of us has a choice: Will I do my work mindlessly and grudgingly, or will I do it out of love?

I remember that my mom chose the latter. When I was growing up, my family would sit down for a meal, and as she was putting the food on the table, Mom would often say, "You know, it's got my secret ingredient: *love*." My brother and I would roll our eyes and tease her for making such a corny statement, but she was actually doing it right. Love really is the "secret ingredient" that transforms our mundane actions into everlasting gifts of glory.

Now, as for the breadwinners of the family, those who "bring home the bacon," well, as those phrases aptly imply, they also are feeding the hungry and giving drink to the thirsty. Going to work every day and earning the wages that buy the food for your family is an act of mercy. I remember coming to realize this truth one day when I went to work with my dad.

From the time I was a little kid, my dad drove a cement truck, helping to build "half of Los Angeles." Shortly before his retirement, when I was on break from college, I asked him if I could ride along with him in his cab. He seemed happily surprised by my request, checked with his boss, and gave me the thumbs-up. So, the next day, we got up at 2:15 a.m., drove to work, hauled the cement, worked on the jobs, and continually cleaned the truck. In the midst of it all, a new appreciation for my dad suddenly dawned on me.

At one point, as we were bouncing around on a hot, smog-filled freeway with a full load of cement, I remember telling him, "Dad, you know, every cell in my body exists because you've worked your butt off to earn the money that bought the food that I've been eating for the last twenty years." He replied, "You got that right!"

Yep, I got it right. My dad's decades of labor fed the hungry: me. And it was a work of mercy that he'll be rewarded for in heaven, a work of mercy every breadwinner and homemaker will be rewarded for, provided they do it out of love.

Relating that story about my dad reminds me of another father who is dear to my heart: Fr. Leszek Czelusniak, MIC. "Father Lesh," as we call him here in the United States, is a breadwinner and homemaker in a very literal sense. As a priest in the Marian Fathers of the Immaculate Conception and a missionary in Rwanda, Africa, he continues to serve in the aftermath of the horrific 1994 genocide that saw the systematic massacre of nearly a million Rwandans in just one hundred days (20 percent of the country's population). Since the killings, he and his fellow Marian missionaries have lived a rather intense life of mercy, caring for orphans, rebuilding homes and schools, encouraging forgiveness, feeding the hungry, and giving drink to the thirsty.

Regarding feeding the hungry, Fr. Lesh once remarked to a visitor on a humanitarian trip from the U.S. that the children he serves love bread, but "they only get it about once a year." Shocked by this statement, the visitor decided to do something. With the support of his local community in Wisconsin, including a donation of one hundred thousand dollars from the Green Bay Packers football team, he didn't settle on buying bread for the town of Kibeho, Rwanda. Rather, he and the Marian Fathers built a bakery and trained the people how to use it. Now the children in the town and beyond have bread not just once a year but *every day*. It's no surprise, then, to hear that the children beam with joy as they eat their daily bread—it may also be no surprise that the same season the Packers made their donation, they won the Super Bowl.

Now, Father Lesh didn't stop with the bread. Knowing that Kibeho, like many towns in developing parts of the world, does not have a safe and adequate water supply, he traveled to the Midwest to ask several Marian-run parishes for more help. After seeing the photos of the schoolchildren of Kibeho, who had to walk several miles just to get a pitcher of water, the kids at All Saints Catholic School in Kenosha, Wisconsin, responded. They held a Walking for Water fund-raiser in the parking lot of their school and raised enough money for Fr. Lesh to purchase two 2,642-gallon water tanks to catch rainwater for the schoolchildren he serves in Rwanda.

So, there are many ways to feed the hungry, and every one of us, from burly Super Bowl champs to little kids in grade school, can get involved. I hope you'll find a way that works for you.

---

Fr. Michael Gaitley, MIC, is a member of the Congregation of Marian Fathers of the Immaculate Conception. He is the author of *You Did It to Me: A Practical Guide to Mercy in Action*, from which this chapter was adapted.

*"Whoever drinks of the water that I shall give him will never thirst; the water that I shall give him will become in him a spring of water welling up to eternal life."*

*JOHN 4:14*

# 3

# GIVE DRINK TO THE THIRSTY

**HOW FAR DO YOU NEED** to go to satisfy your thirst? The answer for almost a billion people in the world is four miles a day.

# SURPRISING MERCY

*CHRISTOPHER WEST*

Thank God there are few living in the United States who suffer from lack of access to drinking water. Our physical thirst is quenched, but what about the deepest thirst of our hearts—for love? It's from this perspective that I want to speak about the merciful act of giving drink to the thirsty and point to Saint John Paul II's Theology of the Body as a critical gift for our time in teaching us how to receive this mercy ourselves and show it to others.

The Latin word for *mercy*, *misericordia*, means "a heart which gives itself to those in misery." Our world today exhibits a veritable dessert of misery related to our failure to understand the true meaning of love and how our sexuality is meant to express that love. Pope Francis' oft-quoted description of the Church as "a field hospital after battle" couldn't be more fitting in our post–sexual revolution world.

When marriages are crumbling and children are growing up without both a mother and a father; when idealized and hyper-eroticized images of the human body have become our cultural wallpaper and people are valued only if they are accordingly stimulating; when the gross distortions of hard-core pornography have become our main reference point for understanding sexual behavior, and sexual addiction masquerades under the banner of liberation; when the blessing of fertility is considered a curse to be eliminated and the innocent human life that springs from sexual union a threat to be exterminated; when governments institutionalize gender confusion and insist the sexual difference has no real meaning; when parents refuse to identify their children at birth so they can "choose their own gender identity" later in life; when society glorifies those who mutilate their bodies so they can "become" the other sex and vilifies those who raise warning flags; and when our Christian parents, teachers, pastors, and confessors are largely unable to respond to these challenges in any compelling way for lack of proper formation themselves, we are a deeply, deeply wounded people.

"I see clearly," said Pope Francis, "that the thing the Church needs most today is the ability to heal wounds." And this means that "ministers of the Church must be ministers of mercy above all."[2] Ministers of mercy are those willing to enter into the pain and misery of people's lives, touch their wounds, and surprise them with tender, healing love. Think of how the bishop in *Les Misérables* treated Jean Valjean when he stole his silver. *That's* the kind of "surprising mercy" that heals wounds and changes the course of human lives.

Yet, as Pope Francis laments, many people in search of healing, rather than being met in their need by true "ministers of mercy," are met by ministers of the Church who are either "too much of a rigorist, or too lax. Neither is merciful," Francis explains, "because neither of them really takes responsibility for the person. The rigorist washes his hands so that he leaves it to the commandment. The loose minister washes his hands by simply saying, 'This is not a sin' or something like that. In pastoral ministry we must accompany people, and," Francis insists once again, "we must heal their wounds."[3]

*Accompanied.* Mercifully *accompanied.* That's how I felt when I first encountered St. John Paul II's Theology of the Body. I didn't know how this Polish pope knew so much about the inner movements of my heart, but I knew his teaching—not "too rigorist" and not "too lax," but carefully balanced and piercingly beautiful—was "healing my wounds" and setting me on a course of true healing.

With John Paul II's help, I was coming to see why Christ was so compassionate toward sexual sinners, especially women: Jesus knew that behind their deception, they were thirsting for him, the true Bridegroom. Think of the woman caught in adultery (see John 8:2–11). She went looking for love, intimacy, union with another, but, as always, the counterfeit couldn't satisfy. Laden with shame, she was brought before Christ by an angry crowd anxious to stone her. Christ then said whoever was without sin could cast the first stone. According to his own words, the sinless Christ could have thrown a stone, but Jesus came not to condemn. He came to save (see John 3:17).

St. John writes that "Jesus was left alone with the woman" (John 8:9). That must have been the moment she felt at her depths the true Bridegroom's heart of love and mercy—a heart that gave itself to her in her misery. Do you think when Jesus said, "Go, and do not sin again" (John 8:11), she turned and grumbled, "Who is this man to tell me what I can and cannot do with my body"? Or do you think, having encountered the love she had been looking for all along, she left transformed and affirmed in the deepest part of her being as a woman? That's the power of mercy.

What are the lies you have believed about your body, about the bodies of others, about the meaning of gender and sexuality? What are the distortions you have bought into? What are the wounds you have endured because of your own folly and the folly of others? Take up a study of St. John Paul II's Theology of the Body and you will discover that behind all the sexual pain and confusion in the world and in our own hearts is the human thirst for heaven gone awry. Sexual sin, you might say, is a quest to satisfy our thirst for heaven with "dead water." Christ meets us right there with his mercy: "If you knew the gift of God . . . you would have asked him and he would have given you living water" (John 4:10). But, like so many of us, the woman at the well didn't know the gift of God, so she had taken her thirst elsewhere: "You have had five husbands, and he whom you now have is not your husband" (John 4:18). Six lovers. Do you see the symbolism? Six is the imperfect biblical number. Seven is the perfect biblical number. Who is this woman's seventh "lover"? Christ, the Bridegroom! His love is what she's been thirsting for the whole time—a "living water" welling up to eternal life (see John 4:1-36).

How tender Jesus is with our broken humanity! We must not be afraid to throw our wounded selves wide open to Christ, to invite his healing, merciful love to come into all the diseased images we have of our bodies and our sexuality, so that he can heal our wounds and transform us into the men and women we are truly created to be. Our hemorrhaging world is crying out for this merciful love. The need couldn't be more urgent. For such a time as this have we been given

St. John Paul II's Theology of the Body. Take up a study of it and let Christ's mercy ever more deeply into your own wounded humanity so that you can become a living witness to the well of Christ's "living water" for others.

---

Christopher West is the founder and president of the Cor Project and the bestselling author of *Fill These Hearts.*

# REFRESHING MERCY

*LISA M. HENDEY*

As our dusty four-wheel drive hits yet another cavernous pothole along the winding road, I consider the half-full plastic water bottle in my hand. Gazing across the Tanzanian countryside, I ponder whether or not to take a sip. I'm parched in the high humidity, but I have no idea when our next stop will take place. My middle-aged mental precautions are on overdrive. In all honesty, I'm more concerned with whether I'll need to use the facilities than I am with being thirsty. Since the local water is strictly off-limits for our small band of journalists, our drivers have cool bottled water at the ready to keep us hydrated.

After I tuck the bottle back into my well-equipped pack, my eyes spot her. That first day on the road, I marvel at her slight build and the mammoth brightly colored bucket atop her head. She looks ahead as she walks up the hill, as strong and beautiful as a ballerina. In each of her hands is a basket, and at least twenty liters of water balances perfectly on the scarf that covers her hair. She'll walk a few miles without becoming winded and likely won't spill a drop.

By my guess, she is probably twelve years old, and I immediately wonder why she's not in the village school we just passed. In my head, I name her Neema, after the beautiful Tanzanian staffer who will be our guide for the week as we travel with Catholic Relief Services. Our four-wheel drive passes her at highway speed and I am in awe of the strength, both mental and physical, that it must take Neema to carry out this chore every day.

Our week in Tanzania unfolds. My days are littered with countless "Neema" sightings as our driving routes take us across diverse landscapes. Despite altitude and vegetation changes, these young girls and their head-borne buckets are a constant. I learn that according to the United Nations, across Africa 90 percent of water collection duties fall to women. Many of them in Tanzania, like Neema and her fellow girls under the age of fifteen, are statistically less likely to attend school; instead they work to gather water, wood, and food for their families.

In ways I never could have imagined, my travels in Africa have helped me to appreciate Christ's command to "give drink to the thirsty." Even before witnessing water being carried along roads in Tanzania, I had a startling "water moment" the previous year in Rwanda in a mountaintop village. Our hosts for a celebratory event had invited us to "freshen up" at a place of honor in their complex of hutlike homes. As VIPs, we had the opportunity to use a special handwashing station that had only recently been built with CRS support. Cleansing our hands in that simple outdoor basin helped me realize how often I stand idly with my tap running. On that Rwandan hillside, I gave thanks for the ability to wash, as well as for the work that had gone into making this simple task possible.

Over the past few years, my gratitude for the simple blessing of water has grown exponentially. I reside in California's Central Valley, where droughtlike conditions have us conserving this precious resource. While our brown lawns and shorter showers have left some of us feeling like we're sacrificing, the opportunity to mindfully conserve has reminded me again that water is a luxury. In the day that it will take me to write and revise this reflection, more than two thousand children will die from diarrhea caused by unsafe water and poor sanitation. It's hard for those of us with ready access to all of life's basic necessities to comprehend that close to a billion people worldwide live without access to safe water. When we do stop to learn the facts, it becomes much easier to combine our small sacrifices with humble acts of giving to ease this worldwide problem.

As a result, when I ponder Christ's preaching on the works of mercy in Matthew 25, my mind goes immediately to water, to access, and to sanitation. I know from my work with relief agencies that every dollar we spend on this problem yields a quadruple impact in productivity and health.

Yet I have also come to believe that as followers of Christ, our commission to "give drink to the thirsty" extends far beyond the literal. Yes, we can and should work together to create a world where girls won't have to forgo education in favor of lugging endless buckets of water on their heads. Yes, let us each make small sacrifices to ensure proper sanitation so that another precious preschooler isn't lost to an excruciatingly painful death from diarrhea.

But let us also remember that the "thirsty" often have needs that will be met more often by words and deeds than by water. I don't have to travel halfway around the world to find folks who thirst. They are all around me, waiting for me to bear relief to them just as Neema bore that bucket of water.

The thirsty are the working poor of my own community who labor in farm fields to put food on their tables. My elderly neighbor *thirsts* for someone to sit with her and to simply listen. A friend who single-parents a child with special needs *thirsts* for compassion, understanding, and welcome. And often, my own family *thirsts* for my care and attention when I let my daily busyness stand in the way of lovingly fulfilling my vocation as wife and mother.

Christ knew the thirsty too. We read in John's fourth chapter that Jesus encountered one of them, a Samaritan woman, at a well. To her, even in her sinfulness, he brought the healing love of "living water," a promise of eternal life. Who among us hasn't witnessed this scriptural moment of conversion and wished it for ourselves? Yet those of us who know and love Christ by merit of the saving waters of our baptism are offered this very same promise. And as believers, a portion of our "Yes, God" to the creator who loves us so dearly is to be "thirst quenchers" to a world very greatly in need of the hope we know in Jesus.

We have the boundless gift, but also the tremendous responsibility, to become the hands, feet, and *yes, even the heads* that bear the living water to those in need. When I am giving God the very best of myself, I am Neema, carrying that bucket filled with Christ's love up that lonely winding highway. Even when the conditions are terrible, the load feels too heavy, and the recipients are ungrateful, this is my job:

to give drink to the thirsty. Just as Neema and her friends love and serve their families and communities day after day, Christ, who daily quenches my thirst, calls me to the same blessed commission.

Sometimes the "drink" we carry to those who thirst will be literal. Often, it will be figurative. Regardless, let us pray daily for gratitude for those who have quenched our thirst and for the grace to carry the drink of living water to those most in need.

---

Lisa M. Hendey is the founder of CatholicMom.com and the bestselling author of *The Grace of Yes*.

*"He who has two coats, let him share with him who has none."*

*LUKE 3:11*

# 4

# CLOTHE THE NAKED

**WHAT IF YOUR BROTHER DIDN'T** have a coat to keep him warm this winter? What would you do to make sure he got one? Well, your brothers and sisters in Christ are out there right now without proper clothing to satisfy a legitimate need.

# GIVING MERCY

*DR. ALLEN R. HUNT*

Clothe the naked.

In the corporal works of mercy, Jesus calls us to do something—not simply to talk about it, not to study it, not to establish a committee to develop a plan for it, but to do it. To really and truly clothe the naked.

Why? Because, Jesus says, when we clothe the naked, we are clothing *him*. In other words, we just may see the eyes of Jesus himself in the face of the person we clothe. Not only will a person find warmth and dignity in clothing, but we ourselves will also be transformed by the grace of God in the process.

Clothe the naked.

Generous followers of Jesus do just that.

---

Mike and his nine teammates from work spent a week in South Africa, focused on feeding the poor. They went to a new village each day to share helpful, more efficient ways to grow food so that the local residents might prosper. In those visits to rural villages, Mike's team encountered in real faces the AIDS epidemic and its ravaging consequences on families and individuals. In that country alone, about 2.5 million children have been orphaned by the AIDS virus, and Mike met dozens of them each day in the villages—kids raising themselves and often struggling to raise their younger siblings.

On the last day of their visit, the team spent a day at a facility devoted to serving the needs of orphans and widows. Half the campus housed orphans; the other half, elderly women in need. As the team circulated through the residents, they played soccer with the children and listened attentively to the life stories of the widows. On this, the final day of their compassionate trek to South Africa, they engaged with fellow humans living in dire need.

When the day drew to a close, the teammates gathered together to head to the airport and return to the U.S. As they stood by the van and shared with one another their experiences from the day, they were quickly surrounded by the children and elderly women, who were grateful to have been noticed and valued, even for one day. Then, Mike noticed something. None of the adults or children were wearing shoes. He suddenly felt an overwhelming urge to take off his boots and give them to a resident of that facility.

In one final act of kindness in a week that had been filled with them, the team spent its last hour in Africa with each of its members seeking a local resident who wore about the same shoe size as the American.

As the van pulled away to head to the airport, ten people now had shoes to wear, and the American teammates were wearing large smiles . . . and bare feet.

**Share. Clothe the naked.**

When my friend Denise had cancer, a group of us took turns driving her to chemotherapy treatment. On the assigned day, a friend would arrive at her home by seven thirty a.m., help her to the car, and then transport her to the doctor's office for the first round of chemotherapy, administered at eight a.m.

It was a humbling process for everyone—for Denise, as she slowly lost her hair and endured the physical indignities and suffering that come with cancer and chemotherapy; and for the friends who accompanied her in their own small ways, driving, praying, and gently encouraging her on the journey. Life becomes very fragile in a chemotherapy clinic.

On one of her first trips to transport Denise, Lisa sat in the waiting area and read during the hours Denise was receiving her treatment. In the corner of the doctor's office, Lisa noticed a box filled with knit winter caps, what we in the South call a "toboggan."

At two different times while Lisa was waiting for Denise, a nurse came into the waiting area and led a chemotherapy patient to the box. They laughed as they sifted through the large selection of caps until the patient found one she liked, tried it on, and took it home with her.

When this happened the second time, Lisa asked the receptionist about the box of knit caps. The reply surprised her.

"In the Catholic parish down the road, there's a group of women who like to knit. And one of them decided a few years ago that no cancer patient should ever have a cold head. So, the ladies bring a batch of new caps by every few weeks to be sure that each patient here knows that someone really and truly cares."

I've never met those knitting ladies, but I know what they look like. They look a lot like Jesus.

**Knit. Clothe the naked**.

---

For years, the Reyna family has had a Christmas Day tradition. Once the presents have all been given, opened, and celebrated, each member of the family takes a few minutes to go to his or her closet and gather items that have not been worn at least once in the past year. Each person then folds the selected slacks, shirts, and coats, and places them in a bag. On the day after Christmas, Mr. Reyna takes the family's bags of clothing and delivers them to the St. Vincent de Paul Society center so that what has not been worn in the past year by the Reynas can be worn in the coming year by someone who needs it.

However, as the years have passed, Mr. and Mrs. Reyna have decided to take it one step further. Their income and financial comfort have increased. They've also noticed that the gifts they give to their children have been based less on their needs and more on their wants.

As a result, several years ago, the parents made a decision. They would still have the family gather unworn clothing each Christmas Day. But from then on, for every dollar they spent on Christmas clothing for their children's gifts, they would give a dollar to the St. Vincent de Paul Society. And as their children have grown older, the parents have invited them to do the same. In other words, every dollar in gifts to their own family is matched with a dollar to assist another family in need.

The Reynas hope to teach their children not only to notice the needs of other families but to recognize those needs as equal to their own. Sacrificing to make a Christmas gift is designed to do just that: help the recipient while transforming the giver.

**Sacrifice. Clothe the naked**.

---

How will you respond to Jesus' invitation to clothe the naked? You might start by picking one of these three words: *Share. Knit. Sacrifice.*

"Come, you who are blessed by my Father. Inherit the kingdom prepared for you from the foundation of the world" (Matthew 25:34).

---

Dr. Allen R. Hunt is a speaker and bestselling author at The Dynamic Catholic Institute.

*"I was sick, and you visited me."*

*MATTHEW 25:36*

5

# VISIT THE SICK

**THERE IS NO SUBSTITUTE FOR** human interaction. You can send a gift, make a phone call, write a letter, even say a prayer, but nothing compares to a smile and a hug. Nothing says "you matter," "you have dignity," "you are loved" quite like a personal encounter.

# DIVINE MERCY

*FR. DONALD CALLOWAY, MIC*

Mercy: We all need it. In fact, St. John Paul II repeatedly described divine mercy as *the* answer to the problems of the world.[4] The great news is that God wants us to receive his mercy. Jesus himself told St. Faustina: "The greater the sinner, the greater the right he has to My mercy."[5] In his papal bull, *Misericordiae Vultus* ("The Face of Mercy"), Pope Francis says that mercy is "the bridge that connects God and man, opening our hearts to the hope of being loved forever despite our sinfulness."[6]

However, receiving mercy is just the beginning. We must also do our part. As Pope Francis said, "[W]e are called to show mercy because mercy has first been shown to us."[7] He reminds us that in the Gospel of Luke, Jesus told us to "Be merciful just as your Father is merciful . . . for the measure you give will be the measure you get back" (Luke 6:36–38). He goes on to say that we will specifically be judged on the corporal and spiritual works of mercy we perform.

St. Thomas Aquinas too specified that we *must* perform acts of mercy, standing in the Catholic tradition that teaches we are duty-bound to perform works of mercy by the natural law (do unto others as we would have them do to us) as well as by the direct command of Jesus in the Beatitudes in Matthew 5:7: "Blessed are the merciful, for they shall obtain mercy."

Following the Gospels, Pope Francis says that it is his "burning desire that . . . Christian people may rediscover and act on the corporal and spiritual works of mercy."[8] One of the corporal works of mercy the Holy Father lists for us to perform is to "heal the sick." Now, you might wonder how you can heal the sick if you are not a medical professional. The good news is that in the *Catechism of the Catholic Church*, that same corporal work of mercy is noted as "visiting the sick" (*CCC*, 2447).

Another translation of this work of mercy is to "comfort" the sick.[9] In all cases, the first step is reaching out to those in need. Whether they are physically ailing or "sick at heart" from social isolation, being forgotten, or missing the basic human need of friendship, just a visit can be healing. One beautiful aspect of this corporal act of mercy is that it does not require wealth, research, skills, experience, or even travel: There are lonely people near most of us in nursing homes, hospitals, and long-term care facilities.

You might still be wondering what you should do when you visit the sick. I know I did. I remember during my first year of seminary, I was on vacation and a neighbor came over and said that his elderly mother was on her deathbed. My neighbor asked me if I could "do something." I told him I wasn't a priest yet, but that I would be more than willing to visit with his mother. I really didn't know what to do other than spend time visiting and praying with the family. What I discovered when I got there was that she was not at peace because she had not lived a holy life. My response was to turn to the Divine Mercy Chaplet and pray it by her bedside. Since the family did not know how to pray it, I prayed it out loud. What happened next was amazing. Right in front of all of us in the room, the dying woman went from torturous agony and fear of death to a peaceful and happy countenance. Immediately after the Divine Mercy Chaplet was finished, she passed away. I can't help but think that the Lord took her soul to himself with a loving embrace at that very moment. To this day, the encounter remains one of the most powerful events I have ever experienced. It proved to me that visiting the sick and praying the Divine Mercy Chaplet for them is extremely powerful.

Just being present and praying is all that is needed. Visit, sit with the person, and pray. That's all there is to it! Jesus himself asked the same of St. Faustina: "Pray as much as you can for the dying. By your entreaties [that is, insistent prayers] obtain for them trust in My mercy, because they have most need of trust, and have it the least."[10] He also said that when we say the Chaplet of the Divine Mercy in the presence of the dying, "I will stand between My Father and the dying person, not as the just Judge but as the merciful Savior."[11] "At the hour of their death, I will defend as My own glory every soul that will say this chaplet; or when others say it for a dying person, the indulgence is the same."[12] St. John Paul II recognized the awesome power of this prayer by imparting a special apostolic blessing "to all the faithful who, during Adoration of Our Most Merciful Savior in the Most Blessed Sacrament of the altar, pray the Divine Mercy Chaplet for the sick and for all those throughout the world who will be dying in that hour."[13]

As important as the Chaplet of the Divine Mercy may be, it is not the only way to help the sick and the dying. Each of us has special gifts. On one occasion, after I was ordained as a priest, a man asked if I had the time to visit his sick mother and anoint her because she was near death. I did not have my holy oils with me, so I went to a local church, where the pastor allowed me to use his holy oil. I discovered that the elderly woman was a devout Catholic, wore a scapular, went to daily Mass, and prayed the Rosary faithfully every day. Her faith was extremely edifying to me. During my visit, she informed me that she always knew that a priest would come to anoint her as she lay sick, preparing for death. She told me that she had even observed the First Five Saturdays devotion, which focuses on making reparation to the Immaculate Heart of Mary. For those who observe this devotion, Our Lady made the promise that they would not die without having received the graces necessary for salvation. I was practically in tears as the elderly woman told me this story and how she had known a priest would come to her. I was that priest! Our Lady was faithful to her promise, and I felt honored and privileged to have been the one called upon to perform this work of mercy for a sick person.

It is so inspiring to hear the many ways people visit with and heal the sick—spiritually, emotionally, and physically. Pope Francis has laid out our task; it is up to us to share this same love we have received from God with others. In fact, this is the very definition of mercy! Mercy is a particular mode of love, such that when love encounters suffering, it takes action to do something about it. It is making someone else's pain our own. Mercy is *love in action*. And there is no better way to put our love into action than to visit the sick and share with them our love (received from God).

There are many ways in which you can reach out and share your mercy with the sick and the dying. For instance, volunteer with a Meals on Wheels program to deliver meals to homebound individuals and visit with them while they eat. Or you can ask your parish priest if he knows of fellow parishioners who would welcome a visit. Sometimes they are even closer to home, so do not forget about members of your own family who might need a visit, or even just a call or an e-mail to show that someone is thinking about them.[14]

We all know that visiting the homebound, elderly, or chronically ill can be challenging at times. It takes many of us out of our comfort zone and can be both physically and emotionally draining. This is where you have a real opportunity, because not only are your presence and your willingness to be a friend and to listen precious gifts that mean far more to them than you can imagine, but you too will receive a gift beyond measure. You will grow in the virtue of compassion, and have the satisfaction of knowing that you made a difference in someone's life. Without being a medical professional, you visited, you healed, and you gave comfort!

---

Fr. Donald Calloway, MIC, a convert to Catholicism, is a member of the Congregation of Marian Fathers of the Immaculate Conception and the author of several books, including *No Turning Back: A Witness to Mercy.*

*"The Spirit of the Lord is upon me, because he has anointed me to preach good news to the poor. He has sent me to proclaim release to the captives and recovering of sight to the blind, to set at liberty those who are oppressed."*

*LUKE 4:18*

# 6

# RANSOM THE CAPTIVE

**WOULD YOU WANT TO BE** defined by the worst thing you have ever done? God doesn't want that for you either. The only sin that can't be forgiven is the one you never ask forgiveness for. Redemption is for everyone.

# FREEING MERCY

*KERRY WEBER*

The chaplain from San Quentin State Prison sat down in my office, and I began to pour my heart out to him. Fr. George and I had met about a year earlier in California, but I hadn't seen him for some time and so was glad to get a chance to catch up. In particular, I was eager to tell him—or anyone who asked, really—about my recent trip to Rwanda. I'd traveled there with Catholic Relief Services to report on the country's 1994 genocide and the healing and reconciliation that had taken place since.

Beginning in April 1994, over the course of one hundred days approximately one million people were killed in Rwanda. Most of the victims were members of the Tutsi ethnic group, a minority in the country, killed by members of the Hutu majority. Much of this killing took place among neighbors, people who had spent time with one another in their daily lives. And so I told Fr. George about how, for years, CRS worked with the people of Rugango Parish and the diocese to create the Community Healing and Reconciliation Program, which fostered discussion and forgiveness among people of that community—a community where survivors and perpetrators of the genocide lived side by side.

I told him about the individuals I'd met there, including Esperance and Fidele. Fidele had killed several members of Esperance's family during the genocide. He told us that when he realized the grave evil he'd committed, he went to Esperance to ask for forgiveness. Esperance told us, "When they said I could meet the person who killed my husband and family, I didn't want to meet them. But he came to ask me forgiveness. I told him, 'If you ask from deep within your heart, I forgive you.'"

And these two individuals spoke of this not sitting on opposite sides of the room or across a discussion circle, but sitting side by side, their hands intertwined, just as their lives were now inextricably bound. And then they hugged.

"I am a genocide survivor," another woman, Viviane, told us. "It was difficult to forgive." And yet she managed not only to forgive, but to help a man named Boniface, the man who had harmed her, as well.

"I was in prison ten years," said Boniface. "Because of the crime I did, my conscience urged me to confess and ask forgiveness. During the genocide, I destroyed her house, but when I came out of prison, I learned that she was living in peace and harmony with my wife. She helped my wife to feed me in the prison. Another member of the community, I killed his relatives and he also forgave me, and we live in peace. He assists me in my poverty. Today we are united and together we focus on the future."

Of course, all this was a gradual process. And still, the group continues to reach out to other members of their community. They have participated in discussions and they take part in "solidarity activities" during the annual month of mourning each April. They also listen to other traumatized people, and helped to build a home for a woman outside the community. The parish also has formed a youth club, which helps to educate young people for peace.

One survivor told us, "We forgive because we know God also forgives." And that forgiveness offers both parties a chance to heal. Boniface later said, "I can't express how I feel in my heart after being forgiven. It was a kind of rest. I had it heavy on my heart."

When I finished my stories, Fr. George looked at me and thoughtfully said, "You should come to San Quentin." He then told me about the restorative justice program there that many men participate in. It's a program in which the men seek healing and forgiveness for their crimes and from victims, family members, and themselves. He said the men there would appreciate these stories. When I objected (I don't know enough; I'm no expert, I told him), he told me to bring the stories, to simply be a conduit for these grace-filled examples.

And so I found myself standing in front of about eighty men in the San Quentin prison chapel and unsure of how my talk would be received. I didn't know if they would want to hear of the violence and pain in the stories I brought, given the violence and pain they'd experienced or perpetrated in their own lives. I didn't know if they would be interested or bored or angry. And I certainly didn't expect the kind, polite welcome that greeted me.

I told the stories of the men and women I'd met in Rwanda, and the men in the California prison sat quietly and attentively. They listened intently and asked intelligent questions. They were thoughtful and kind. They readily shared from their own lives and talked about the painful divisions, some gang related, that had caused them problems. They were eager to talk about forgiveness, to try to move forward, to move on, to remember. They shook my hand and spoke about their prayer lives.

And there, in the middle of the prison, in this place so purposely cut off from the rest of the world, I felt a part of a community. It was a community that included both the men beside me and the men and women I'd met halfway around the world, all of us struggling, suffering, seeking forgiveness. All of us trying to become better. And I felt then that the true power of such community is in the way we accompany one another in this struggle. We are meant to accompany each other, as Christ accompanies us. We carry each other. We urge each other. We encourage each other. And one of the wonderful parts of being in a merciful community is that our fellow community members are able to see things in us that we might not see in ourselves. Others may see gifts or talents that we possess that we might not be willing to acknowledge. They see our faults too. We help each other stay on the right path when we can. And even in our imperfection, our own brokenness, we can help others heal. Together, and with the grace of God, we are lifted up, let out, set free.

---

Kerry Weber is the managing editor of *America* and the author of *Mercy in the City: How to Feed the Hungry, Give Drink to the Thirsty, Visit the Imprisoned, and Keep Your Day Job.*

*"Precious in the sight of the Lord*
*is the death of his saints."*

*PSALM 116:15*

7

# BURY THE DEAD

**HAVE YOU EVER BURIED SOMEONE** you deeply care about? What if you couldn't do that? What if you couldn't honor those you love? What if you couldn't have that closure? It is a great act of mercy to bury the dead and show reverence for them at their grave site.

# HOPEFUL MERCY

*MOTHER OLGA YAQOB*

Every year on Good Friday, we pray with the old traditional hymn "Were You There When They Crucified My Lord?" For a lot of us, it is a very familiar and memorable hymn because we grew up with it in our Catholic tradition.

Though it is traditionally and historically very true, none of us today, outside the sacrifice of the Mass, can go back to Calvary and meet the Lord there. However, throughout the years of my vocational path and ministry, I have come to learn that through both the corporal and the spiritual works of mercy, the Lord has led me to his Calvary. There I have come to encounter his pierced heart, touched many of his wounds, and held his dead body by caring for the wounded of war and burying the dead in my homeland, Iraq.

I was a teenager when the first war started in my country, which took eight years of my upbringing as a young woman. In the midst of the darkness of violence, hatred, bloodshed, and deaths of both civilians and military personnel, faith in God became my anchor in the face of such a storm. His words became the compass that guided me during such a confusing time when many people lost their faith and purpose in life. At such a young age, the words of the Lord in Matthew 25:35–40 about giving food to the hungry, clothing the naked, visiting the sick, welcoming the stranger, and attending to the prisoners, were not only a service to others but also a much deeper encounter, in which Jesus invited his followers to see him in those whom they served: "Truly, I say to you, as you did it to one of these least my brethren, you did it to me." This passage became the motto that radically changed my life and directed my vocational path throughout my ministry until today.

Throughout the four wars in Iraq, from 1980 to 2003, I met Jesus in his Calvary through many works of mercy, including visiting the sick, serving the elderly, caring for the prisoners, and bringing food and medicine to the homeless. One of the most difficult and painful aspects of that Calvary was being at the foot of the cross and witnessing the most critical wounds in the final hours of individuals' lives, both those who were sentenced to death in underground prisons for political reasons and those who died in the street because they had no one left after the many wars that took the lives of their families and loved ones. Burying the dead at such a young age became a call within a call for me. I turned to the Virgin Mary, who stood at the foot of the cross when they took down the body of her only Son and laid him in her arms, that precious body, beaten, pierced, and covered with blood. I turned to her to help me ponder with her heart such a mystery of carrying that many broken, bloody, wounded, and unclaimed bodies. They were very difficult times in my life. I had to take responsibility for bringing their bodies to our convent to wash them according to the custom of the culture in order to prepare them for burial.

At one point, we had to pick up a homeless man who had died on the street. His skin was all covered by bugs, and on some parts of his body, his wounds were open and his bones were exposed. By the time we arrived at the convent, nobody was able to get near his body to wash him and prepare him for burial. As I prepared the water and the soap and approached to wash him, I suddenly smelled a strong aroma of incense coming out of his wounds, and I called the sisters and the volunteers to come near him to smell it. Nobody could smell the incense. Yet for me, it was very strong. I knew at that moment it was the Lord confirming for me his words in the Gospel of Matthew that he spoke to me in my teenage years, that it is truly him we meet in those whom we serve.

Shortly before Christmas Eve, when our community was praying with a dying person who was put on hospice care, I felt the presence of the Blessed Mother, sorrowful yet full of hope as this man was dying and moving on to eternal life. Since it was a few days before Christmas, his favorite season, our sisters began singing Christmas carols. During that time his wife asked me to help her with changing him. As I was doing so, I helped her to hold his very weak and frail body, which was so worn from a long battle with cancer and months of treatment. I felt the presence of the Blessed Mother again carrying this poor broken body on the threshold between earth and heaven. I felt her heart, which had held the body of her Son on Good Friday yet believed that the Resurrection Sunday was coming. Her sorrowful heart and hopeful spirit gave me the strength to be with this family whose father died on Christmas morning, and she continues to guide my ministry of burying the dead and helping families during their time of grief and loss.

Through my ministry with young people, I have come to witness a different kind of death and grief—a spiritual one. Today we find in our culture many people who are spiritually poor and unfortunately at times perhaps even spiritually dead. The effects of sin and ignorance on faith and morality can be very dangerous to the lives of individuals, leading to confusion and poor choices, which harm the soul. Unfortunately we all know families and individuals who have been impacted by such darkness and loss. Here too I find my way to Calvary, through the spiritual works of mercy of instructing the ignorant, comforting the afflicted, and helping those who might have been at the edge of spiritual death to come back to life and allow themselves to be found by God, who is not only the source of life but also the giver of grace for those who seek new birth in Christ through the sacrament of his mercy. I have seen the birth of such life in young women who came to the fountain of mercy after suffering from abortion and in young men who came seeking healing after being wounded in the darkness of pornography and addiction.

Yes, it is painful to be at Calvary, yet because there I meet Jesus, the one who is the life and Resurrection, even when I'm there to bury the dead or walk with those who are spiritually dead, I stand there with hope, to carry hope, and to pass on hope.

---

Mother Olga Yaqob of the Sacred Heart, founder and mother servant of Daughters of Mary of Nazareth, was born and raised in Iraq.

# PERSONAL MERCY

*SR. MARIE VERITAS, SV*

*You matter*. When everything boils down, that is what this work of mercy—burying the dead—is all about. We, as human persons, are both fleshy and spiritual, nitty-gritty and infinite, body and soul—a meeting of the material and spiritual worlds. Just think—there was a time when you *were not*. And then, in an instant, you *were*. In that moment when God loved you into being, he cried out with infinite delight: "He is *very* good. . . . She is *very* good" (Genesis 1:31). But he didn't stop at simply creating you in his image and likeness. Just as at the baptism of Jesus in the Jordan, when *you* were baptized into Christ, the voice of the Father spoke over *you*: "You are my beloved son [daughter], with you I am well pleased . . ." (Mark 1:11).

The Christian practice of burying the dead as a work of mercy is based on this twofold sacredness of the human person, created and redeemed. In coming face-to-face with this twofold holiness, we encounter the ultimate reality of who we are: beloved sons and daughters of the Father, temples of the Holy Spirit, unique and unrepeatable, in need of redemption and destined for glory. That's why it's a big deal to bury those who have died—because their lives mattered and continue to matter. Death doesn't end the story.

Now, let's be honest—most of us are not gravediggers, funeral home directors, or morticians. How does this work of mercy apply to us? Unless we have to, many of us might even "skip over" burying the dead altogether because of its unpredictable timing and its strange, sorrowful, sensitive, and even frightening nature. But when we look at Scripture, we see that *the body is a big deal.* My body is *me.* Our bodies have the capacity to communicate the truth about our dignity and destiny. And that's a big deal. So big a deal, in fact, that Tobit risked arrest and death to bury the bodies of his kinsmen (see Tobit 1:17). So big a deal that the Word became flesh in Mary's womb (see Luke 1:38). So big a deal that when Mary of Bethany anointed Jesus before his passion, Jesus said: "She has done a beautiful thing to me. . . . She has done what she could; she has anointed my body beforehand for burying. And truly, I say to you, wherever the gospel is preached in the whole world, what she has done will be told in memory of her" (Mark 14:6, 8–9). Looking closely, we see that this work of mercy actually hits home in the most intimate place of our hearts: our deep thirst to know that even our greatest vulnerability—death—doesn't take away the meaning and purpose of our bodies.

Death is a consequence of sin (see *CCC,* 1008). God did not intend death for us, but when our first parents signed the sin contract, so to speak, death became a sort of family inheritance. The resurrection of Jesus rocked the universe by turning death on its head, to the point that Christians now look at a tomb as the definitive sign of hope and ultimate mercy. "The limit imposed upon evil—[upon death]—is ultimately Divine Mercy."[15]

Mercy draws good from evil. It is the love that does not allow itself to be conquered by evil, pain, or suffering, but overcomes evil with good. Jesus took on, in his burning love for us, our entire human experience, in order to redeem it. He became flesh so that our flesh could become him. St. Maximilian Kolbe, a Franciscan priest who was imprisoned in Auschwitz during World War II, knew this firsthand. He was assigned to cart the bodies of the deceased to the crematoriums, and could be heard whispering over and over as he did so: "*Verbum caro factum est*" ("The Word became flesh"). In the mangled bodies he was forced to transport, Kolbe saw the body of Jesus, who took upon himself all of our suffering, pain, and death and gave us the resurrection in return.

Now, sometimes we might mumble over the part of the Creed that says: "I look forward to the resurrection of the body . . ." Hold on. Whose body, exactly? Here's the wild thing: Yours. Mine. After we die, on the last day, our bodies will be raised up through the power of the resurrection of Jesus. He said it himself: "This is the will of my Father: that everyone who sees the Son and believes in him should have eternal life; and I will raise him to life on the last day" (John 6:40). This ain't no zombie movie, folks. This is real, bona fide mercy in action. It is the Lord promising us that his mercy is infinitely greater than any darkness, sin, death, or decay. There is nothing, absolutely nothing beyond the love and mercy of Jesus, and he wants the whole you—including your eyes, nose, ears, and the way your hair does that funny thing in the morning—to be transformed, purified, and glorified with him forever in heaven. When we really believe this, we live differently, because we see that our bodies are not shed like snakeskin at death. Rather, in death, our bodies, separated from our souls in the ultimate poverty and powerlessness, await Someone who will come and bring this body back to life.

That's why, in our modern "throwaway" culture, the Church has to be very specific regarding cremation, permitting it as long as it is not an intentional action of disbelief in the resurrection and the ashes are interred intact in a sacred burial space. That's also why the Church makes a point to venerate the relics of the saints, because their bodies retain a connection with their souls.

But let's talk nuts and bolts. What can we do to practice this powerful work of mercy? Some simple ideas include: attend wakes and funerals whenever possible; visit cemeteries; bring flowers to grave sites; visit those who are grieving. Burying the dead is a mercy not only to those who have died, but to those who mourn their loss. When circumstances make it impossible to acquire someone's body for burial—as in the case of war, or those who have suffered after abortion and have entered the healing process, or someone who has donated his or her body for research—it can be powerful to create a memorial for that person.

Burying the dead is an act of faith in the resurrection of Jesus, and an act of charity, mercy, and reverence toward the person who has died. In burying someone we are saying: "You are worth reverencing. You are sacred. And you belong to Christ." With this act, we surrender to the earthshaking reality of the truth of ourselves, body and soul, and the mad love God has for us.

*Behold! I tell you a mystery. . . . We shall all be changed, in a moment, in the twinkling of an eye. . . . For the trumpet will sound, and the dead will be raised imperishable, and we shall be changed. . . . When the perishable puts on the imperishable, and the mortal puts on immortality, then shall come to pass the saying that is written: "Death is swallowed up in victory. O death, where is thy victory? O death, where is thy sting?"* (1 Corinthians 15:36–55)

---

Sr. Marie Veritas, SV, is a Sister of Life based in New York.

# AFFIRMING MERCY

*DR. CAROLYN WOO*

In looking over the seven corporal works of mercy contemplating this article, I was, of course, reminded of their links to one of my favorite chapters in the Bible: Matthew 25. Here is found the origin of what Mother Teresa would call the "Gospel of One Hand," putting out her fingers as she counted off the words: "You did this for me."

In that chapter, Jesus at once establishes and reminds us of this simple, profound concept: Since God is found in every person, how we treat our neighbor is also how we treat God. This is at the foundation of why the Catholic Church in the United States formed and supports the overseas humanitarian agency Catholic Relief Services (CRS), which I am privileged to lead. Our faith tells us that our neighbors are not just in our neighborhood, or in our town or city or state or even country; they are found all over the world. All of us are brothers and sisters in God's family of mankind.

In Matthew 25:35–36 we find the queries and instructions from Jesus that became the foundation of the corporal works of mercy: "For I was hungry and you gave me food, I was thirsty and you gave me drink, a stranger and you welcomed me, I was naked and you clothed me, I was sick and you visited me, I was in prison and you came to me."

But as I read on in the works of mercy, my eyes landed on the one that is not in Matthew 25, the last of the seven: to bury the dead.

This might seem odd, as the work of CRS is certainly among the living. All that we do is aimed at nourishing, sustaining, and supporting life, from the moment of conception with our prenatal programs, to childhood education and nutrition, to helping adults with agriculture and livelihood, all the way throughout our years on this earth.

Each and every day, working with local partners and friends in countries around the world, we carry out so many of the works that Jesus enumerated in Matthew 25—feeding, clothing, and giving drink and shelter. It is our gospel mission that follows from the works of mercy.

But still this last instruction kept resonating with me. Archaeologists tell us that the presence of rituals accompanying the burial of the dead is one of the earliest signs of the development of civilization. These rituals show the beginnings of an awareness of our humanity, of our special place in God's creation.

Such rites can speak eloquently to the roots of so many ills that plague us today, the same kinds of issues that Pope Francis addressed in his encyclical on the environment, *Laudato Si*. After all, the dead have no intrinsic value in the marketplace. They cannot contribute to the bottom line. Dealing with them reverently and respectfully only increases inefficiency.

Pope Francis lets us know in his encyclical that such thinking—looking on everything in God's creation, including people, as nothing more than pragmatic commodities—is an essential part of the attitude and actions that have led to the appalling treatment of the common home that God has given us, the natural world that is our earth.

When we take time out to bury the dead as the works of mercy ask of us, we acknowledge the importance of the living. This body is not a useless object; it is a holy vessel that carried a soul whose resurrection is the wondrous promise of redemption. With our rites of burial, we are affirming that life is more than physical matter, that it is a gift from God for which we must always be humbly grateful.

Our goal is to help people loosen the shackles of poverty so that all may live the lives of dignity that God intended for them. The appropriate treatment of the dead affirms this dignity as surely as a bountiful crop, a good education, proper nutrition, a decent house, clean water, and proper health care.

Let me tell you about what happened in 2014 in the West African country of Sierra Leone as it was being devastated by an outbreak of the deadly Ebola virus. Ebola is a horrifying illness spread through contact with the secretions of those who have it. The disease does not die with its victims; their bodies are highly contagious. In West Africa, handling the bodies of the dead was one of the main ways the virus was spreading.

The order went out from the public health authorities to the people of Sierra Leone: Do not touch the bodies of your loved ones. It ran completely counter to the traditions of these communities, where reverential care for the dead was expected. This included tenderly washing the body to prepare it for burial. Sadly, this was just the kind of contact that was most dangerous. It led to many deaths.

Faced with this vile epidemic threatening the health of so many, the authorities in Sierra Leone responded with perhaps understandable urgency. At a report of a possible Ebola death, a team dressed in protective suits descended on the household, sprayed the body with disinfectant, put it in a plastic bag, and removed it from the presence of those in mourning. The suits meant that those handling the corpse had no contact, either with the body or with those in the household.

The result was widespread distrust of these authorities. People began hiding the dead, not reporting the deaths. In secret they carried out their time-honored funereal traditions, thus, tragically, spreading the deadly virus.

Relief workers began coordinating with the public health institutions as well as with local spiritual leaders to come up with an alternative approach. So instead of a team in off-putting garments arriving unannounced, someone would visit the family and explain the situation, the proper way to pay respects and avoid contamination. This person would be followed by those who would actually handle the corpse. Though wearing the protective equipment, they would act with appropriate respect. The body would be treated properly. The relatives would know its destination and fate. They would be allowed to express their grief and love in ceremonies that resonated with their beliefs.

This extra care resulted in a tremendous increase in those cooperating with the health authorities and thus a huge decrease in the rate of infection. It was a critical element in bringing the Ebola outbreak under control in Sierra Leone.

It is probably true that few members of the relief team that worked on the burial-with-dignity project in Sierra Leone knew they were carrying out one of the seven corporal works of mercy. But they did know they were working in a manner that affirmed the dignity of those we serve.

This time, in the midst of this horrific epidemic, it was only by ensuring the dignity of the dead that we affirmed the dignity of the living—certainly a worthy work of mercy.

---

Dr. Carolyn Woo is the president and CEO of Catholic Relief Services.

# PART TWO

# THE SPIRITUAL WORKS OF MERCY

*"Blessed be. . .the God of all comfort,*
*who comforts us in all our affliction,*
*so that we may be able to comfort those who*
*are in any affliction, with the comfort*
*with which we ourselves are comforted by God."*

*2 CORINTHIANS 1:4*

8

# COMFORT THE AFFLICTED

**EVERYBODY IS GOING THROUGH SOMETHING.** Sometimes they need a hug. Sometimes they just need someone to listen. Sometimes they need a shoulder to cry on. Will you be that friend?

# COMFORTING MERCY

*LISA BRENNINKMEYER*

When I sat down next to my friend after the funeral reception was over, the raw pain in her eyes tore into my heart. She had just lost her teenage daughter. Christmas would never again be the same for her. There would always be an emptiness in the midst of the festivities. My friend's story was heavy with pain. When despair and depression had become overpowering, when the pain had felt unbearable, her daughter had made the choice to end her life. So we sat, with just quietness between us. After a few minutes, she looked around the room and spoke words that I believe hold a message for the body of Christ.

"You know, this isn't my church. This isn't where I had planned to have the funeral. But when we called the church to tell them what had happened, they said they'd come to us, but they never did. If you are ever going to show up and *be the church*, that time was now. That time was this week for my family. Their silence spoke loudly to us. So we decided to do the funeral somewhere else. It was just too painful to be in a place where they obviously didn't care about us."

I don't believe my friend's church doesn't care. Most likely someone dropped the ball entirely by accident. Perhaps a note with my friend's name and address had been caught by a draft and fluttered away. It's very unlikely that anyone proactively decided to ignore this hurting family at such a critical time. But what I really wonder is where was the safety net of the church *community*? Why were their arms not wrapped tight around this family? They could have run interference, helping bridge the gap between who the church wanted to be and what the family was experiencing.

Affliction comes in many forms. We don't wear our heartache as visible, outward wounds, but we all know how much pain is out there. In the midst of a sin-saturated world, people need to know that they matter, that their pain matters, that they are seen. It's been said that suffering that feels senseless is the hardest to bear. When that is compounded by a feeling that the pain must be carried alone, despair can quickly set in. But what a difference the presence of a comforter can make. We can't answer all the questions about the suffering, but we can say, "I see it. And most important, I see you. I won't let this pain swallow you or overwhelm you."

Isn't this the message of the Incarnation? Bridging all distance between God and man, Jesus moved into the neighborhood. He reached out and touched the leper, looked into and healed the eyes of the blind man, and restored Peter when his heart was overwhelmed with his own failure. He rushed in when there was pain instead of recoiling or standing back where it felt safe.

Isn't this the example that the Blessed Mother gave us? She didn't shrink back from human suffering. She didn't shield her eyes when her Son was stripped, beaten, and crucified. She pressed into the suffering and stayed by his side, providing strength with her presence.

This is how we are asked to live.

"Comfort, comfort my people, says your God" (Isaiah 40:1). These words aren't just for our priests and parish staff. They are spoken to you and to me. God promises in Isaiah 43:1–2, "Fear not, for I have redeemed you; I have called you by name: you are mine. When you pass through waters I will be with you; and through rivers, they shall not overwhelm you; when you walk through fire you shall not be burned, and the flame shall not consume you." One of the ways that God fulfills this promise to his people is through the hands and hearts of his children. He understands that while his presence makes all the difference, we also need a human hand to grasp hold of. We need to see eyes that understand and don't judge. What a privilege it is that he trusts and calls us to be a part of this ministry of comfort.

Nothing makes us more effective ministers of comfort than having suffered ourselves. Not one of your tears of pain will be wasted if you allow them to be redeemed in the life of another. God can use every ounce of what you have been through to make this world a better, kinder place. In 2 Corinthians 1:3–4 we read, "The God of all comfort. . . comforts us in all our affliction, so that we may be able to comfort those who are in any affliction, with the comfort with which we ourselves are comforted by God."

If you have experienced miscarriage, divorce, grief, abuse, financial crisis . . . could it be that God is calling you to step out and encourage others who are going through those very things today? You are uniquely equipped to offer comfort because you have been there. You understand. You are proof that life does go on. You are a carrier of hope.

This is the call to the body of Christ. We are to surround one another, to press into one another's pain, to offer the gift of our presence. Sometimes sitting silently alongside someone is the best gift we can give. Sometimes it's making a meal. Sometimes advice is truly helpful. The important thing is that *we show up*. That we slow down enough to notice the pain in someone's eyes. That we ask questions, and then wait for the answers. There is no Christmas present under the tree that will have the kind of life-changing impact that the gift of our comforting presence offers.

*Lord, open our eyes to see the invisible wounds people carry. Help us to look through grace-healed eyes that search deeper, that pause, that step closer when an aching heart is near.*

---

Lisa Brenninkmeyer frequently speaks to women's groups and is the author of *Walking with Purpose*.

# TRIUMPHANT MERCY

*CURTIS MARTIN*

All alone in the suffocating summer heat of India stands a young girl. Her energy is failing as she swats at the flies swarming around the dozens of open wounds on her body, the result of untold insults to her innocent life. The crowds press on without taking the slightest notice of her appalling condition, until a small group of college students come around the corner and encounter her in her poverty. These eight students are on a Catholic mission trip. Not quite sure what to do, they look around to see if a mother or father might be nearby, and it quickly becomes apparent that the girl is by herself.

They offer her some water. The young girl appears to be disoriented and frightened by these newcomers, but her thirst triumphs and she accepts the water, gulping it as if she were drinking for the first time in days. As they sit with her, they are distracted by the multitude of open wounds on her tiny body. One of the students is a nursing student with some basic medical supplies. As they clean and dress the wounds a crowd begins to gather, filled with curiosity. In a nation where beliefs in reincarnation and Karma are prevalent, the idea of helping someone in distress is an oddity. The local beliefs hold that if people experience hardships in life, it is because their previous life must have been a bad one. They need to "work it out for themselves." Outside of Judeo-Christianity, the harsh reality is that acts of kindness to those in distress are a novelty. The conviction that we ought to comfort the afflicted is a unique hallmark of Christianity, which all too often we may take for granted.

In fact, comforting the afflicted is not just an aspect of the Christian life; in a certain way, it is the defining characteristic of Jesus Christ and (ought to be) of those who follow him. At the heart of the Catholic faith is a God who looks with love upon the children he has created. He sees in us the devastating afflictions sin has caused, and he enters into the drama of our lives to join us and to comfort us. His mercy meets us in the here and now and leads to everlasting life.

For followers of Jesus, comforting the afflicted is not so much a set of good deeds that we are obliged to perform as it is a revelation of the true nature of the world that God has created, redeemed, and saved. Christians behave differently because their faith leads them to see everything differently. Christians comfort the afflicted because they have discovered the true meaning of life. They come to understand that what they have freely received they ought to freely share.

For nonbelievers, there is enough evidence to conclude that the world is an essentially brutal place, where the innocent and weak not only suffer, but suffer at the hands of the strong. They believe that Darwin was right and only the strongest and the fittest will survive. Jesus came to reveal a radically different perspective, a deeper truth, a more powerful truth: that suffering, while real, is not the final word.

He reveals that love and mercy triumph. Jesus Christ's very life demonstrates that infinite love, not unbridled power, is the essential meaning of the universe.

When those who follow Jesus seek out the afflicted and comfort them in their misery, they are revealing the very heart of God, who is rich in mercy (see Ephesians 2:4). To take notice of needs and afflictions is the first step of mercy. To step out of my own needs and my own preoccupation and take notice, and then to move into another's life with comfort, is not only a revelation of the nature of the universe and the God who freely chose to create it, it is also the key to unlocking God's mercy in our own lives. Jesus taught us, "Blessed are the merciful, for they shall obtain mercy" (Matthew 5:7). So, in addition to bearing witness to the true nature of the universe, acts of mercy open up the floodgates of mercy in our own lives.

This is critically important for each of us, because the death of Jesus upon the cross shines light into our lives. We are told that "for the joy that was set before him endured the cross" (Hebrews 12:2). What was the cause of Christ's joy that enabled him to endure the cross? First, that you are worth it. He died for you personally, so your life must be worth immeasurable value. Second, that what he gained for you must be worth it. What awaits you in heaven must be of unimaginable worth. Third, that you need more help than you thought necessary. Most of us know that we are not who we are meant to be. We deceive ourselves, though, into thinking that if we just tried harder we might be able to close the gap between who we are and who we ought to be. It is almost as if we think we need a spiritual workout, or a spiritual aspirin. Yet Jesus reveals from the cross that we are radically broken and in need of profound mercy. His death (and resurrection) is the only effective remedy for our gap. His mercy is the perfect response to our misery.

This is great news—or what the Bible calls the "gospel," literally the "good news"—that we need mercy and that God so loves us that he gives us his mercy, so that we can be who we are meant to be, and so that we can be with him forever. To share good news is what the Catholic Church calls "evangelization." It is simply letting people know that even on their worst day, they are loved, and that the God of the universe wants to comfort them in their affliction. The appropriate response is to accept God's mercy, and then manifest that mercy by comforting others in their afflictions.

The Catholic Church, we are told, "exists in order to evangelize . . . it is her deepest identity."[16] If this is true, what does it mean? The heart of Catholicism is to rejoice in God's mercy and share our joy, in words and deeds. Evangelization is an introduction to God and his loving mercy. Incredibly, through God's amazing love, Christians don't just receive mercy; we are transformed by it. By God's grace we become like him and just as we have personally received mercy, we can ourselves go on to comfort the afflicted. As (then) Cardinal Ratzinger wrote, "In the end, evangelization means to set out with Christ in order to pass on the gift we have received, to transform poverty of every kind."[17]

---

Curtis Martin is the founder and CEO of FOCUS, the Fellowship of Catholic University Students, and the author of *Made for More*.

*"Let your speech always be gracious, seasoned with salt, so that you may know how you ought to answer every one."*

*COLOSSIANS 4:6*

**9**

# INSTRUCT THE IGNORANT

**TAKE A LOOK IN THE MIRROR.** Examine your conscience. Do you practice what you preach? Pope Blessed Paul VI rightly proclaimed, "Modern man listens more willingly to witnesses than to teachers, and if he does listen to teachers, it is because they are witnesses."

# SHARING MERCY

*SARAH SWAFFORD*

Whenever I would read through the corporal and spiritual works of mercy, it always gave me pause when I came across "instruct the ignorant." The sweet Kansas farm girl in me would think, "Gosh, that's not very nice. It's pretty harsh to call someone *ignorant*." Upon delving deeper, I found that my modern-day connection to the word *ignorant*, meaning "dumb" or "rude," was actually not at the heart of this work of mercy.

*Ignorant* is from the Latin meaning "not knowing." It can also mean "unlearned," "unknown," or even "unaware." When you think about this work of mercy as asking us to instruct the "not knowing" or "unaware," our task becomes clear and, dare I say, exciting.

In our modern age of transmitting information at the speed of light, or more accurately, at the speed of an Internet connection, it can easily feel like we are constantly bombarded with information. Almost any question can be answered fairly quickly (as my children like to request, "Just google it, Mama!"), but when it comes to questions such as, "How do you know there is a God?" "Why does the Church teach that?" and "I know they say it's morally wrong, but what if I feel it's right?"—even Siri can be at a loss for words.

Being a member of the Holy Catholic Church instituted by Christ more than two thousand years ago can sometimes feel like drinking from a fire hydrant. Our heritage is rich with teachings from the Scriptures, *Catechism*, encyclicals, works of the saints, and countless other phenomenal resources at our fingertips. And while we should always be learning, growing, and deepening our own faith, we also know we are called to share these amazing truths with others, and that is no small task.

In my own life, I have found the work of mercy of instructing the "not knowing" or "unaware"—instructing the ignorant—to be a mix of exhilaration, frustration, excitement, and terror all rolled up in one. To share one's faith with family, friends, coworkers, or complete strangers can be intimidating, and it's easy to feel immense pressure to say the "right thing" or have the "perfect argument" for the thousands of questions someone could ask.

In light of trying to dig deeper into this work of mercy, instruct the ignorant, I think it would be beneficial to distinguish between knowledge and wisdom. Knowledge is very important; we should have the facts and information we need to communicate the brilliant truths of our Catholic faith. But someone may have all the factual knowledge in the world—he or she may even be a "walking *Catechism*"—yet unless we approach this work of mercy with an eye to imparting *wisdom*, we may very well miss the mark.

It is wisdom and faith that take knowledge and seamlessly weave it through the threads of time, history, culture, and personal experience in order to help answer life's biggest questions: "Who am I?" "What am I living for?" and "Whom am I living for?" Wisdom and faith are the anchors of human life, giving us meaning and purpose even amid the attacks of relativism, utilitarianism, and the culture of death. Wisdom and faith show us that life has a plot, a goal, and living out this journey leads to happiness, peace, and joy—both in this life and in the next.

I have seen firsthand that nothing is more critical to the human person than making these truths one's own—for when one loses purpose and meaning in life, one quickly falls into despair. The willingness to communicate wisdom, faith, purpose, and meaning in life is an act of love that heals the deepest of wounds and poverties: the sadness and loneliness of thinking life is not worth living.

We will all be called upon at one time or another to impart "facts" and knowledge about the truths of our faith. But as the saying goes, "More is caught than taught." Communicating this spiritual and Christian wisdom is a way of life, not merely a memorized lecture; it touches the head and the heart and therefore transforms the whole person—intellectually, spiritually, morally, and emotionally. To instruct the ignorant in this way requires a life of witness; it requires that we radiate the love, peace, and joy that Christ has lavished upon us—and only in this way can we authentically communicate it to others.

If we think of instructing the ignorant as an overly cerebral enterprise in which we are worried about having a flawless argument or making sure we have the perfect answer to every accusation against our faith, then this work of mercy could sound smug or even condescending; but if we understand the deeper purpose of knowledge (namely wisdom, and ultimately faith), we then see that this work of mercy aims at nothing short of communicating the love of God to every person we meet. Each person has been willed into existence by God and each person has a unique part to play in the grand story of human life in light of the cross. Instructing the ignorant aims to help each person find his or her role in this great story of salvation, giving him or her meaning and purpose—and ultimately a mission to do the same for others.

I love to meditate upon the lives of the early Christians, and especially the lives of the apostles. When I feel overwhelmed, anxious, or unqualified to instruct the ignorant—the not knowing or unaware—I think back to a story from Acts 3. Peter and John were going to the temple and saw a beggar who had been crippled since birth lying at the gate: "And Peter directed his gaze at him. . .and said, 'Look at us.' And he fixed his attention upon them, expecting to receive something from them. But Peter said, 'I have no silver or gold, but I give you what I have; in the name of Jesus Christ of Nazareth, rise and walk'" (Acts 3:4-6).

The man was healed that day, and as he leaped in front of the temple praising God, all the people were filled with wonder and amazement. The line from Peter, "I give you what I have," is something to meditate on. We may not always have the perfect answer or argument, but we have the same truth, knowledge, wisdom, faith, and conviction that was given to the apostles; the same Holy Spirit descends upon us and asks us to go out to all the nations and tell the Good News (see Matthew 28:19-20; Acts 2:1-6). We have found our role, our part to play in the story—and remember, no one can argue with your story, your testimony.

We have been given a gift greater than gold or silver. If we would give drink to the thirsty, clothe the naked, ransom the captive, and give bread to those who are hungry, how much more should we give them the Bread of Life when they hunger and thirst from the utmost depths of their being?

---

Sarah Swafford lives in Atchison, Kansas, and is the author of *Emotional Virtue: A Guide to Drama-Free Relationships.*

# ENDURING MERCY

*SR. MARY MADELINE TODD, OP, STD*

Thirty-one: It is not just the number of days in the longest months of the year. It is the number of times the direct address "Teacher" (in Greek, *Didaskale*) is used in the Gospels. Seven: It is not just the number of days in the week. It is the number of times "mercy" (the Greek noun *eleos*) occurs as a concrete reality in the Gospels. Some say that every great preacher or teacher has only one message and that every sermon, speech, or lesson conveys that one truth. For Gandhi, it might be peace; for Dr. Martin Luther King Jr., we might say it is freedom; for Mother Teresa of Calcutta, it could be service. For Jesus Christ, the message could assuredly be summarized as love. We could rightly observe that love is the key to the message of all four of these famous teachers, for how can we build a society of peace, freedom, and service without love? Yet one could argue, and convincingly, that one particular aspect of love lies at the heart of all the teaching of Jesus Christ: mercy. Mercy is, in the life and teaching of Jesus, *the* manifestation of the love God has for humanity and of the love each person is called first to receive and then to give.

In teaching, while a clear message calls for unity, a strong method calls for diversity. Effective teachers instruct not by one technique, but by many: presenting foundational principles, applying those ideas to concrete situations, asking learners to practice what has been demonstrated, and ultimately living or embodying the truth. Jesus masterfully summarized the principles of the Christian life in the Sermon on the Mount. Among the attitudes he proposed as truly blessed was that of being merciful, proclaiming, "Blessed are the merciful, for they will obtain mercy" (Matthew 5:7). When in that same discourse he taught his followers to pray, he again emphasized the essential link between the need for mercy *from God* and the showing of mercy *to others*, as he included in the Our Father the request, "Forgive us our trespasses, as we forgive those who trespass against us" (Matthew 6:12). Knowing how important repetition is, Christ the Teacher added commentary to the prayer, explaining, "If you forgive men their transgressions, your heavenly Father will forgive you. But if you do not forgive men their trespasses, neither will your Father forgive your trespasses" (Matthew 6:14–15). Later in Matthew's Gospel, Jesus replied to those criticizing him for eating with tax collectors and sinners by stating explicitly, "Go and learn what this means, 'I desire mercy, and not sacrifice.' For I came not to call the righteous, but sinners" (Matthew 9:13). When the Pharisees again were looking for fault in his disciples, as they picked grain on a Sabbath to satisfy their hunger, Jesus repeated the lesson: "If you had known what this means, 'I desire mercy, and not sacrifice,' you would not have condemned the guiltless" (Matthew 12:7).

Jesus not only directly and repeatedly stated the need to be merciful, he also used the most poignant of his parables to illustrate the beauty of God's mercy for us and of our mercy toward our neighbors. His tale of the prodigal son has never lost its power to convey the desperation of the son's need for mercy in his state of wasted riches and rejected sonship and the greatness of the father's compassion. Even while his son is a long way off, the father catches sight of him, runs to him, embraces him, and kisses him. Instead of chastising his son with words of rebuke, the father calls for a celebration, rejoicing that his son has returned to his family and his home, to the love that sought him even when he did not want to be found. In this parable, Jesus illustrated not only the tenderness of the Father's mercy but also the goodness of the mercy that can radiate from a human heart that has received divine mercy. Even mainstream culture uses the phrase "good Samaritan" to praise the person who, like the man in Jesus' story, seeing a neighbor in need, does not simply pass by, but rather stoops to uplift and care for the one who is beaten, robbed, and abandoned on the road. Jesus' portrait of the true neighbor as one who shows mercy still resonates today.

Beyond instructing his listeners about mercy, Jesus called them to apply mercy in the concrete situations of life. At dinner with Simon and some Pharisees, Jesus welcomed a woman who was judged in the minds of others as a sinner, and therefore as undeserving of notice and forbidden from contact. She was full of sorrow and deeply desirous of the mercy that she saw in the gentle face of Christ. She humbly anointed his feet, only to be condemned by the self-righteous Pharisees. Jesus invited Simon to learn the truth that the woman had already mastered, the profound link between love and mercy. Contrasting Simon's inhospitable actions with the superabundant attentiveness of the women, Jesus said to him, "Therefore I tell you, her sins, which are many, are forgiven, for she loved much; but he who is forgiven little, loves little" (Luke 7:47). On another occasion, it was once again the scribes and the Pharisees, those who were supposed to be the teachers, who failed to grasp the meaning of mercy. They brought to Jesus a woman caught in adultery. Ready to stone her and hoping to trap Jesus in some misstep regarding the law, they addressed him as Teacher and asked him his interpretation of the Mosaic Law. Jesus' reply, which invited the one without sin to cast the first stone, did not reject the law, but rather transcended an interpretation of it that favored justice without regard for mercy. A master teacher, Jesus called them to apply principles not only to others but also to themselves, to discover the law not as a tool to condemn others, but as a call to be converted.

The greatest lesson of all is the embodiment of the truth one wishes to convey in one's life. Jesus did not merely preach mercy, illustrate it, and call his listeners to pray for and exemplify it; he gave it. From the last pulpit he ascended, that of the cross, where he spoke seven final words, he showed the cost and the glorious triumph of mercy. In the face of betrayal by a friend, denial by a confidant, abandonment by his inner circle, lies by false accusers, rejection by the masses, derision by the teachers, and violence by unjust captors came his reply: "Father, forgive them, for they know not what they do" (Luke 23:34). His mercy endures forever. Has ever a lesson been so well taught and yet so often forgotten? May we remember it, thirty-one days a month, seven days a week, every day that we live.

---

Sister Mary Madeline Todd, OP, STD, is a Dominican Sister of St. Cecilia Congregation and an assistant professor of theology at Aquinas College in Nashville, Tennessee.

*"And convince some, who doubt."*

*JUDE 1:22*

# 10

# COUNSEL THE DOUBTFUL

**HAVE YOU EVER BEEN IN** a state of doubt? If so, then you know it is an extremely vulnerable place to be in. The only cure is Jesus. Think of St. Thomas when he exclaimed, "My Lord and My God!" Clarity is a rare but powerful commodity.

# EMPOWERING MERCY

*JACKIE FRANCOIS-ANGEL*

I grew up Catholic, and so the word *mercy* became a part of my vocabulary at an early age. At every Sunday Mass we would repeat after the priest or deacon, "Lord, have mercy. Christ, have mercy. Lord, have mercy." The readings would often speak of God's mercy toward his people, and the priest would say the word multiple times during the Liturgy. Then, a few moments before we received Jesus in the Eucharist, we would sing, "Lamb of God, you take away the sins of the world, have mercy on us."

While I may have said and heard *mercy* many times in my life, I never really took time to reflect on the word's meaning. To me, *mercy* just meant that I was a sinner and God was kind and merciful enough to forgive me. My teenage, Orange County, California-born and raised, nonchalant Catholic response to God's mercy was more of a "Cool! Thanks, God! I guess you're *supposed* to be nice, so of course you're going to give me mercy if I ask for it."

When I was eighteen, the Lord crashed into my life in a big way, changing my lukewarm heart to a heart on fire for him. While my speech, dress, and actions all changed, one of the biggest changes came with my intellect. I started reading and learning more about the Catholic faith. I had merely gone through the motions for the first eighteen years of my life, but then the fire in my heart built a desire to really know God more through spending time with him at daily Mass, reading Scripture, and reading Catholic books like crazy. I started listening to Catholic CDs and podcasts, and going to talks. Any way that I could grow, I tried. Many of those Catholic authors and speakers have no idea how much of a spiritual work of mercy they were doing for my heart and mind by "instructing the ignorant." I didn't even know how to pray the Rosary correctly until I was eighteen! One of the most beautiful lessons I learned, though, was all about mercy.

Mercy is one of those theological concepts that seem pretty abstract. I know I have *experienced* mercy from God and from others. I also know there are times when I've been merciful. But I always thought of mercy as just having to do with forgiveness. Even as a music minister and songwriter, I have a hard time finding many songs that sing specifically about what mercy *is*; rather, most sing about mercy in relation to what God has done, or they use the word to describe him.

It wasn't until recently, when I heard a priest's homily about mercy, that I finally had a concrete definition to apply to my thoughts and actions in daily living. This priest broke down the Latin word for mercy, which is *misericordia*, derived from the two words *miserere* ("pity" or "misery") and *cor* ("heart"). He then proceeded to say that when we ask for God's mercy, we are essentially asking him to relieve us of a heart that is in misery. And our hearts can be in a state of misery not just from sin, but from the deep hurt caused by a broken relationship with a family member, from the suffering of infertility, from the pain of a physical or mental illness, from losing a job, from being betrayed or abandoned, from spiritual or physical poverty, and so on.

Now when I think about mercy as "relieving someone from a heart in misery," I realize that I've experienced God's mercy *much* more than I could ever count. And I've also realized that I, in turn, have given mercy to others in more ways than just by forgiving someone who has wronged me.

The seven spiritual works of mercy show that mercy is more than just forgiving offenses willingly; it can also include instructing the ignorant and counseling the doubtful. I have frequently lived out these latter two spiritual works of mercy in my fourteen years as a youth minister and as a speaker at teen conferences. While I'm speaking to young men and women from a stage, most often I'm instructing the ignorant, just as countless speakers have done for me. However, it is afterward, when I get to meet these teens face-to-face, that I get to hear their stories and practice the spiritual work of mercy of counseling the doubtful.

Most people think "giving counsel to the doubtful" means simply giving advice to someone who is having a faith crisis, or perhaps proving the existence of God or the fullness of the Catholic Church to a skeptic. This would be a very limited understanding of this work of mercy. To delve deeper, it helps to know what *counsel* and *doubtful* mean. A priest has helped me with this one too. Msgr. Charles Pope writes:

> *The English word "counsel" comes from the Latin* consilium *(*con *[with] +* silium *[a decision]). . . . So to counsel means to assist*

> *someone in the act of deciding, not just to give vague or generic advice. . . . The word "doubt" comes from the Latin word* dubius *meaning "uncertain." . . . So we have come to a more precise description of the spiritual work of mercy we call "Giving counsel to the doubtful." It is that work which helps the undecided (or those of two minds on something) to come to a good and upright decision rooted in the call to holiness and the goal of attaining Heaven by God's grace.*[18]

By that definition, there are many opportunities to "counsel the doubtful." In youth ministry, I'm often helping young men and women decide to get out of relationships that are leading them away from God. My husband and I help to counsel many single Catholics who are torn in their discernment between consecrated celibate life and married life. I also try to give counsel to teens or young adults who want to become Catholic but have some reservations, whether theological or family related. And, of course, I have tried to help young people make good decisions when they explain they are dealing with very serious issues such as pornography addiction, suicidal thoughts, abortion, cutting, eating disorders, or abuse (and in most of those cases, I refer them to professional counselors or authorities).

In all of these situations (and the millions more that you can think of) in which we are giving counsel to the doubtful, we are actually practicing a spiritual work of mercy by "relieving a heart in misery." And this comes not from us, but from God. It is the Holy Spirit who gives us the gift of counsel, and it is only by knowing God that we can lead others toward him and his will, which is "good and pleasing and perfect" (Romans 12:2). Thus, every time we go to Mass and say, *"Lord, have mercy. Christ, have mercy. Lord, have mercy,"* we know that the God who is relieving us of a heart in misery is also empowering us by his Holy Spirit to go and do the same for others.

---

Jackie Francois-Angel is a full-time traveling speaker, singer/songwriter, and worship leader from Orange County, California.

# BEING MERCY

*SR. HELENA BURNS, FSP*

The second spiritual work of mercy, "counsel the doubtful," has got to be the ugly stepsister of the first spiritual work of mercy, "instruct the ignorant." While "instruct the ignorant" is the pretty, shiny, flashy proclamation of the truth to the hungry, seeking ears and eyes of those who suddenly see the light, "counsel the doubtful" deals with the messy, muddled, gray fallout of those who—for whatever reason—just don't get it. However, "counsel the doubtful" is my personal favorite spiritual work of mercy! Why? We live in a doubtful, skeptical age. As the non-Christian culture becomes stronger and stronger, faith gets weaker and weaker. In the United States, according to the Pew Research Center, one in three millennials now declare "no affiliation" as their religion, even if they were baptized. If it were a religion, the second-largest religion after "Catholic" in the United States would be "lapsed Catholic," with twenty-two million members.

The doubtful are an immense mission field! They are precisely the audience for the New Evangelization proclaimed by John Paul II. "There is an intermediate situation, particularly in countries with ancient Christian roots, and occasionally in the younger Churches as well, where entire groups of the baptized have lost a living sense of the faith, or even no longer consider themselves members of the Church, and live a life far removed from Christ and his Gospel. In this case what is needed is a 'new evangelization' or a 're-evangelization.'"[19]

Who exactly are these doubt-filled souls? It would seem they fall into several categories:

- Those who doubt because they need more *instruction to clarify matters for them*
- Those who generally have a *hard time believing in what they can't see*: God, the spiritual, the miraculous, etc.
- Those who have *agnostic or atheistic beliefs*, but have left a little room for the possibility of God
- Those who are growing closer to or transitioning from another religion or belief system into the Catholic Church and are simply finding *certain truths of the Catholic faith difficult to understand, assent to, or live*
- *Young people* who are calling into question everything they were taught as children
- Those who do not have examples of joyful, devoted, prayerful, hospitable, and charitable believers around them, and who are *starving for witness and fellowship* to strengthen their own faith
- Those who lack discernment and are *easily swayed by false teachers and false teachings*
- And sometimes doubt is more a matter of trust: those people who have a *hard time trusting God*—trusting that God really loves them, that he is really on their side, looking out for them, helping them, willing the best for them, really hearing and answering their prayers.

St. Paul the Apostle took great care with those he called the "weak in faith." He told Christians to bend over backward to accommodate them and not scandalize them. He determined to be "all to all" in order to bring as many as possible to salvation.

To counsel the doubtful requires a tremendous amount of patience. If people are doubtful by nature, they may relapse, over and over—much to their own frustration and that of anyone trying to guide them. If we are in a position to do the counseling, we really need to thank God for giving us a strong faith. Constant wavering can be a real cross.

We do not need a degree in theology or catechetics to counsel the doubtful. We all know that some of the most convincing people of faith have been the simplest individuals we've known. They just love God and their neighbor and live straight from the heart. Counseling the doubtful means not turning away from people's questions, misgivings, or fears. It means being a solid rock in the midst of the storms of others' intellects, wills, and emotions that cause them to be "blown and tossed by the wind" (James 1:6). It means painstakingly researching what we ourselves are unable to answer, in order to explicate and reassure, or simply to find and recommend the very best resources.

Counseling the doubtful can also mean, perhaps, enduring slings and arrows against us, God, and the Church by those doubters who are wounded and lashing out. (Whoops! Now we're in the territory of another spiritual work of mercy: "bearing wrongs patiently.") Instead of having a knee-jerk reaction of taking offense and answering in kind, how about *being* kind? You obviously have a treasure that these people do not. They want what you have. Rebuffing them is propelling them further from what they want and need. Sometimes we also think that we need to "defend" God from or against those who are doubtful. As EWTN's Doug Barry says: "God is a big boy." God *doesn't* need us to defend him, but these hurting doubters *do* need our forbearance. People should be able to say of us: "If your God is anything like you, I want to know him."

If we are secure in our own faith, we won't feel threatened by doubters. If doubters cause us to doubt, we need to humbly acknowledge that we don't know everything and seek out answers ourselves, rather than shut down people who challenge our faith.

Are *we* among the doubtful? If we are, we are obliged to get our doubts resolved if possible and as much as possible. Resolving doubts about God, our personal faith, and the content and practice of our faith is part of forming our conscience. Did we see something in the media (perhaps repeatedly) that stirred up doubts within us? Have we taken the time to pursue authentic answers or have we let doubt silently grow and erode the "pearl of great price" within us?

Former atheist turned evangelizer Jennifer Fulwiler was brought into the faith in great part due to a very persistent and patient Catholic couple who host a Catholic blog. They untiringly answered her inquiries and objections and removed stumbling blocks from her path. What was the result of all that spiritual labor? Jennifer Fulwiler, former atheist turned evangelizer.

Maybe one of the reasons I have such compassion for doubters is that, as a teen, I too doubted God and began to believe we really are all alone in the universe. It was the most painful and empty time of my life. Human beings can experience all kinds of pain, but we rarely talk about a very real unseen pain that wreaks havoc in our lives: *spiritual pain.* The spiritual works of mercy relieve that spiritual pain.

---

Sr. Helena Burns, FSP, is a writer, speaker, and filmmaker.

*"If any one among you wanders from the truth and some one brings him back, let him know that whoever brings back a sinner from the error of his way will save his soul from death and will cover a multitude of sins."*

*JAMES 5:20*

# 11

# ADMONISH THE SINNER

---

**ARE YOU A SINNER?** So am I. That is a good place to begin.

# HUMBLE MERCY

*JENNIFER FULWILER*

I converted to Catholicism from lifelong atheism, and I initially understood my conversion to be a purely intellectual endeavor: I read a bunch of books, realized atheism was wrong, saw that the Catholic Church was right, and then I became Catholic. In my mind back then, it was a short, tidy story.

Through this lens, I thought the third spiritual work of mercy was a breeze. Correcting the sinner—how easy! Those of us who know the truth tell the people who are wrong that they're wrong, they see their errors, and everyone is Catholic by Friday.

Oddly enough, my efforts in this department didn't turn out like I might have hoped. Blunt, argumentative statements never seemed to get through to anyone who was in a state of sin. In fact, the more I mouthed off about other people's missteps, the further I seemed to be driving people away from the Church. My attempts at undertaking this work of mercy didn't feel very merciful at all.

It wasn't until a few years later that I finally saw this work of mercy in a new light. I was talking to a kind priest about a recent failure in the "correcting sinners" department, and he asked me to tell him about the people who had influenced me in my own conversion.

As soon as I heard the question, a memory came to my mind, as vivid as if it had happened that morning. I saw myself sitting in my old college dorm room, surrounded by friends, all of us circled around a telephone. And I began to tell the priest the story of Jerry the telemarketer.

My friends and I were gathering our purses and jackets to head to a party, and we all paused when the phone in my dorm room rang. Caller ID showed that it was yet another telemarketer, so I was tempted to skip it. Instead, I decided to have some fun.

I motioned for everyone to get quiet, and I clicked the speakerphone button to answer. A middle-aged man introduced himself as Jerry, and began asking me about my carpet-cleaning needs.

Using a terrible rural Texas accent, I interrupted him. "I don't believe in cleaning carpets. That kind of thing is against my religion!"

The idea came to me to play the role of a religious zealot—it would be funny if I could get the telemarketer to be the first one to hang up by launching into a hellfire-and-brimstone lecture about how carpet cleaners were from the devil. Boy, wouldn't my friends think that was hilarious—me, the consummate atheist, playing the character of a religious nut!

"Well, I'd never heard of that," Jerry replied. He continued hesitantly, "What is your religion, if you don't mind my asking?"

I winked at my friends. "I'm a Christian, of course!"

"Oh, great," he said. "Where do you go to church?"

That one caught me off guard. I could not come up with the name of a single church, so I stammered, "The, church . . . the Church of the . . . Bible."

He gasped in excitement. "Is that Covenant Bible Fellowship out in Huntsville? With Pastor Mike?"

"Why, yes, it is," I said. "Pastor Mike is just darlin', isn't he?" I was trying to get back to the hilarity of my lecture about the evils of carpet cleaning, but the telemarketer's enthusiasm derailed me again.

"How long have you been a Christian, ma'am?" he asked, then quickly added, "I apologize for the personal question, but it's just a topic near to my heart."

"Well, I accepted the Lord Jesus into my heart and soul, oh, ten years ago," I said, mimicking the types of things I always heard my Christian classmates say. "I, uh, walk with the Lord every day now."

"God bless you," he said. "Just . . . God bless you. That is so wonderful to hear."

I glanced at my friends. My face grew hot and red. This was not the triumphant display of my comedic genius that I had planned.

"I've got to tell you, the Lord has just . . ." He paused. He was getting choked up. "The Lord has just done so much for me."

"Well, how lovely," I said. I turned and looked for the handset to the phone but couldn't find it. We were stuck on speakerphone. Out of the corner of my eye I saw my friends shift uncomfortably in their seats.

"I'm sorry," he said as his voice cracked. "It's just that my life was such a mess. I was an alcoholic. My marriage was practically over. I was so depressed. I thought there was no more hope for me. And the Lord . . . the Lord healed me, healed my marriage. I haven't had a drink in twenty-five months and six days. I could have never imagined that my life could be this good again, and I'm just . . . so grateful. I'm so grateful. You know what I mean?"

No longer feeling like anything remotely close to a comic genius, I abandoned the plan of playing the church-lady role and just tried to get myself off the phone as soon as possible. I didn't know what to say. This poor man didn't know he was talking to a militant atheist, and that a bunch of her atheist friends were listening in.

"Oh, yes . . ." I muttered.

"I'm sorry," he said again. "It's just so good to meet people like you, to come across fellow Christians when you least expect it."

I wanted to crawl under my bed and never come out.

"Listen," he continued, "don't you even worry about any of this stuff I was trying to sell you. That's not what matters. I'll let you go enjoy your evening. Could I just ask you for one thing?"

"Um, sure."

"Would you please pray for me?"

Since this was not the time to reveal that I had never said a prayer in my life, I just mumbled yes.

"I'll pray for you too," he said, his voice brimming with an open sincerity that almost broke my heart. "God bless you, ma'am. God bless you and have a good night."

"God bless you too," I stammered, forgetting to use my fake accent. I hung up the phone in a daze.

I turned to my friends; they were silent. None of them were religious; most were atheists, and we never hesitated to ridicule Christians. But this time nobody said anything. Seeing such a rare display of vulnerability had left us frozen.

In the silence that ensued it was clear that though he was the one who didn't get the joke, it was I who was the fool.

Jerry didn't tell me I was wrong for being an atheist. He didn't give me a bulleted list of every sin I had committed lately. Yet without even knowing it, he performed the third spiritual work of mercy in a far more powerful way: He got his ego out of the way so that I could get a glimpse of the love that filled his soul—and I couldn't help but compare what I saw in my own soul to what I saw in his.

My friends and I stood to leave for the party, the awkwardness still thick in the air. I was the last one out, but before I shut the door I paused and glanced at the phone.

I thought of the warmth that Jerry had exuded, how he seemed to possess a level of hope and joy that was somehow both childlike and wise. I considered my own state of heart in contrast, and it was like gazing upon a stagnant cesspool in comparison to a crystal clear stream.

"You know what I mean?" Jerry had asked after telling me how this God of his had taken a shattered mess of a man and transformed him into the type of person who was so filled with love that he couldn't help but share it with the world, even on telemarketing calls. And as I closed my dorm room door, for a brief moment I wished more than anything that I did.

---

Jennifer Fulwiler is the author of the bestselling memoir *Something Other Than God* and the host of *The Jennifer Fulwiler Show* on SiriusXM. She lives with her husband and six young children in Austin, Texas.

# FAITHFUL MERCY

*DANIEL BURKE*

Not too long ago I waited in deep sorrow as my much beloved stepfather, Mel, passed to his final judgment before God. Before his last pained breath, as he lay in home hospice, the doorbell rang and in came the neighbors. These dear Christians asked permission to speak in private with Mel. They asked if they could share the gospel with him before he died.

Mel gently overruled my mother and waved them permission to speak with him. They talked for some time and then left with deep and obvious sadness because of the imminent loss of their dear friend.

My mother asked Mel, "Why in the world would you let them do that?"

He said softly, "They have taken care of us for years. They have loved us. They earned the right to say whatever they wanted to me. They said what they said out of love." This was a profound expression coming from the heart of a lifelong Jew.

There are many ways to look at how we can effectively reach those who seem to be living outside of a covenant relationship with God. One thing is sure: There is no better way to "admonish the sinner" than I witnessed with these good men and my stepfather.

Unfortunately in an age of 140-character emoting, the kind of profoundly merciful and loving encounter that Mel experienced is becoming more and more rare. The radical polarization and depersonalization of technology has widened the divide between those who have the truth and those who need it.

The effect of this digital age is to move too much of our communication about sin and redemption to an impersonal, terse proclamation issued through the cold, hard medium of digital devices. This often gives the evangelist a false sense of accomplishment as he or she lobs truth bombs at heathens and enemies, yielding nothing but anger, offense, and wounded sinners who are now less rather than more open to the truth.

My parents' Christian neighbors built a bridge of love over which the most important truth Mel ever heard could pass. By contrast, the digital-screen machines and their masters yield far fewer conversions, far fewer souls who go from living a life of sin and destruction to a life of joy and faith in the person and work of Jesus Christ.

It is in this context that we have an extraordinary opportunity to reach those lost in sin and light the path to heaven. When it is dark, even dimly lit bulbs can sufficiently reveal the path to safety. And so it is with us.

The key is to recover what it means to be merciful in our communication of truth. Many loudly declare that the mere proclamation of truth is an act of mercy and love and thus sufficient. Does this perspective square with Scripture? Here are a few passages that we can use as a way to test our approach to communicating truth:

> *And we exhort you, brethren, admonish the idle, encourage the fainthearted, help the weak, be patient with them all. (1 Thessalonians 5:14)*
>
> Are we patient and self-sacrificing with those who need to hear the truth?

> *Therefore be alert, remembering that for three years I did not cease night or day to admonish every one with tears. (Acts 20:31)*
>
> Does our passion for God come through humble tears of love as we communicate truth, or are we cold, demanding, and dispassionate Pharisees?

> *Let your speech always be gracious, seasoned with salt, so that you may know how you ought to answer every one. (Colossians 4:6)*
>
> Are we gracious and careful regarding how we prepare the meal of truth? Is our meal stark and made up only of sound nutrition, or does it mirror the banquet feast of God, which is both nutritious and so appealing that none would turn away to a lesser source?

*And the Lord's servant must not be quarrelsome but kindly to every one, an apt teacher, forbearing, correcting his opponents with gentleness. God may perhaps grant that they will repent and come to know the truth, and they may escape from the snare of the devil, after being captured by him to do his will. (2 Timothy 2:24–26)*

Are we quick to argue and defend without the patience that reflects kindness? Are we gentle and hopeful, relying on the work of God that comes through the authentic and self-giving expression of love and truth?

*Speak evil of no one, to avoid quarreling, to be gentle, and to show perfect courtesy toward all men. (Titus 3:2)*

Do we speak poorly of those who are deceived and in need of the light and work of redemption? Are we courteous and do we avoid a confrontational style that will easily lead to closed hearts and minds? Do we treat communication of truth as a boxing match, or as a sharing of love between friends?

*He can deal gently with the ignorant and wayward, since he himself is beset with weakness. (Hebrews 5:2)*

Do we recognize our own weakness and sin in humility as we work to help others, or do we place ourselves above others as the one who is right and superior? Are we ready to wash the feet of the wayward as Jesus did with Judas, or do we stand above God himself in our refusal of humble service?

*But the wisdom from above is first pure, then peaceable, gentle, open to reason, full of mercy and good fruits, without uncertainty or insincerity. (James 3:17)*

Are we peaceful, gentle, and open to discussion with others? Or are we hard and quick to shut down anything that we disagree with without hearing the heart of the other person? Are we constantly waiting to get to our retort, or do we care enough about others to listen carefully so that we can reach their hearts with the truths that would most likely set them free?

*Always be prepared to make a defense to any one who calls you to account for the hope that is*

> *in you, yet do it with gentleness and reverence. (1 Peter 3:15)*
>
> Are you prepared to gently and reverently reveal what God has done and is doing in your life? Are you deeply aware of your own need for a savior and do you thus recognize and long for the salvation of others? Have you prayed for the one you are seeking to help? Are you in a state of grace so that you are animated by God's love, gentleness, meekness, and power as you speak?

Admonishing the sinner in mercy is the all-important task of helping people understand they are off the path to God and lighting the way back to that path through love and truth. If you are not among the cowardly who love themselves and their comfort too much to speak truth, all you need to remember is this one simple phrase: "Love builds a bridge over which truth can pass." If you build that bridge of love in the way you give yourself to others and the way you communicate truth, you will find profound and consistent success in leading hearts to God.

---

Daniel Burke is the executive director of EWTN's *National Catholic Register* and the author of *Navigating the Interior Life.*

*"Finally, all of you, have unity of spirit, sympathy, love of the brethren, a tender heart and a humble mind. Do not return evil for evil or reviling for reviling; but on the contrary bless, for to this you have been called, that you may obtain a blessing."*

*1 PETER 3:8–9*

12

# BEAR WRONGS PATIENTLY

**ON EARTH, DID JESUS ACT** out of a sense of fairness? No, he acted out of love. For love to endure it must be patient, especially in the face of injustice.

# PREVAILING MERCY

*MATT FRADD*

For the past several years I have worked with men and women who are immersed in the sin of pornography and want to be free. In the battle against pornography—or any sin for that matter—it's crucial that we have patience with ourselves. Without it, we will not persevere long in the battle.

We need to remember that the wounds we have received didn't come about overnight, and the healing won't take place overnight either. It takes time, perseverance, and determination.

"Have patience with all things," urges St. Francis de Sales, "but chiefly have patience with yourself. Do not lose courage in considering your own imperfections but instantly set about remedying them—every day begin the task anew."

Several years ago, as I stood in line for the sacrament of confession about to confess for the umpteenth time a sin I couldn't seem to quit, I began to fear that God's mercy was running out. I didn't doubt that God would pardon a person who turned to him after a life of the most heinous sins imaginable. What I did doubt was that he would continue to forgive me. How many times have I said, "I will never do this again," only to return to that sin like a dog to its vomit (see 2 Peter 2:22).

At that moment, by God's grace, no doubt, I was reminded of the incident in the Gospel of Matthew when Peter approached Our Lord with a question:

> *Then Peter came up and said to him, "Lord, how often shall my brother sin against me, and I forgive him? As many as seven times?" Jesus said to him, "I do not say to you seven times, but seventy times seven." (Matthew 18:21–22)*

Now Jesus did not mean that Peter was to forgive his brother 490 times and then no more. No, rather "seventy times seven" signified perfection and consistency. It then occurred to me, if God's forgiveness is not like that—perfect and consistent—then Jesus was commanding Peter to act in a way that was contrary to the nature of God.

The truth is, God is infinite in all of his attributes. In fearing that God's mercy was slowly evaporating, I was unintentionally making God in my image. If you have ever been tempted to doubt God's mercy as I did, or if you're tempted to do that now, please ingrain the following words from St. Claude de la Colombiere into your brain:

> *I glorify You in making known how good you are towards sinners, and that your mercy prevails over all malice, that nothing can destroy it, that no matter how many times or how shamefully*

*we fall, or how criminally, a sinner need not be driven to despair of Your pardon. . . . It is in vain that your enemy and mine sets new traps for me every day. He will make me lose everything else before the hope that I have in your mercy.*

Regardless of where you have been or what you have done, be at peace. The same God who forgave Moses the murderer, Rahab the prostitute, David the adulterer, and Peter the denier will forgive you also. All you have to do is seek that forgiveness with a contrite heart. The only sin God won't forgive is the one you will not ask forgiveness for.

---

Matt Fradd is a Catholic apologist and speaker.

*"Let all bitterness and wrath and anger and clamor and slander be put away from you, with all malice, and be kind to one another, tenderhearted, forgiving one another, as God in Christ forgave you."*

*EPHESIANS 4:31–32*

13

# FORGIVE OFFENSES WILLINGLY

**THE OUR FATHER IS AN** incredibly powerful prayer. It is also full of wisdom. Pray it slowly, and let the words "forgive us our trespasses as we forgive those who trespass against us" sink deep into your heart.

# SCANDALOUS MERCY

*FR. JAMES MALLON*

"You can't give what you don't have." This truism applies to anything that we would attempt to give, including mercy. To give or show mercy requires on our part that we be possessed of mercy. To be merciful requires that we be full of mercy, and the only way to be full of mercy is to be filled with mercy. A mercy that moves us to forgive all injuries can only flow from a heart that has received this mercy. It is not something that we can conjure on our own, or grit our teeth and bring into reality by force of will. A mercy that forgives all injuries—that is, *all* injuries—is beyond our human capacity and is nothing but the fruit of God's merciful love dwelling in our hearts.

*God's mercy is scandalous.* It is outrageous, it is transformative, and it differs greatly from excusing. Some offenses are excusable; many are not. Mercy is required when we are faced with the inexcusable and tempted to declare those offenses unforgivable.

God's mercy is scandalous because it offends our innate sense of human justice. Quite simply, God's mercy is not fair. I think of the Parable of the Prodigal Son and the poor older brother who quite justly protests the lavishness with which his father welcomes the younger brother home (see Luke 15:11–32). The text is quite clear that the younger brother was motivated not by repentance over his rebellion and rejection of faith, family, and culture, but by self-interest. His was a very "imperfect" act of contrition, as he realized that being a servant in his father's household would provide more creature comforts than his present scenario. His carefully rehearsed apology is smothered by the loving arms of the father, who renders insignificant the self-centered manner of the return of his son, and his many offenses are forgiven as he is welcomed back into the family. That these injuries should be so easily forgiven is humanly unfair and scandalous, and yet it is with this unfair and scandalous mercy that we ourselves have been, or can be, forgiven.

*God's mercy is outrageous.* Jesus tells a story in Matthew's Gospel known as the Parable of the Unforgiving Servant, after Peter has inquired about the number of times he ought to forgive (see Matthew 18:21–35). On a first reading of the parable, there is the obvious point that forgiveness ought to beget forgiveness, but the story really highlights the outrageous nature of God's mercy, and it has to do with the comparable amounts in question. The first servant is forgiven 10,000 talents by his master and then refuses to forgive his fellow servant 100 denarii. A denarii was a daily wage for a laborer, whereas a talent was worth more than fifteen years' wages of a laborer (a total of 150,000 years of labor as opposed to 100 days, or $6 billion compared to $12,000 in today's economy). Because most of us today are not specialists in ancient near-Middle Eastern monetary systems, we miss this essential point that would have made the original listeners laugh out loud. The amount is absolutely ludicrous, and the first servant's plea to his master to be patient while he pays back the sum is comedic. The point: God's mercy is absolutely laugh-out-loud outrageous, and yet it is with this outrageous mercy that we have been, or can be, forgiven.

*God's mercy is transformative.* I think of the similar Parable of the Two Debtors. Jesus tells this parable at Simon the Pharisee's home in Luke 7:40–43 when Simon and the other Pharisees are gathered there. A woman—"who was a sinner"—has entered the house and washed Jesus' feet with her tears, kissed them, and dried them with her hair. She then anoints them with oil as Jesus reclines at supper on a couch. Jesus allows her to perform this scandalous and intimate gesture. Small alabaster jars were often worn around the necks of women who belonged to the oldest profession, thus pointing to the origin of her reputation as a sinner. Alabaster is a very pervious stone, and it was used to emit the scent of perfume. This substance, once used to aid her in her former lifestyle, is now used for a different purpose. Through this parable Jesus teaches us about the transformative power of God's mercy: The servant who has been forgiven more will love more. He also allows the woman herself to turn it into a living parable: She is forgiven, but not because she showed love. Rather, the fact that she has shown such love reveals that she has already been forgiven much. God's mercy is transformative, and it is with this transformative mercy that we have been, or can be, forgiven.

When we receive mercy, we are filled with mercy and will be merciful. There is no shortcut. The key to being free of hurt, resentment, bitterness, and unforgiveness, the key to living out the spiritual work of mercy of forgiving all injuries, is to cry out to God for mercy for our own sins and to experience the scandalous, unjust, lavish, outrageous mercy of God. When we experience this at the depth of our being, it will utterly transform us. Our attempts to hold on to past grievances and harden our hearts to those who have caused us injury will seem to be mere comedy. Indeed, when we contemplate our injuries and those who inflicted them upon us, we see that some may still be inexcusable, but none will be unforgivable.

---

Fr. James Mallon is the pastor of Saint Benedict Parish in Halifax, Nova Scotia, the founder and chair of the board of the JPII Media Institute, and the author of *Divine Renovation: From a Maintenance to a Missional Parish.*

# TIRELESS MERCY

*FR. MIKE SCHMITZ*

Few commands of Christ are more ignored or overlooked than his instruction to forgive others as God has forgiven us. It is not merely that forgiveness is difficult to do; it is that very few people understand what forgiveness really is.

There are stories of incredible forgiveness, stories of those who have released ages-old pain and incredible grief. There are also countless grudges and resentments that many of us take for granted. The truth is, whether the offense is unimaginably large or a daily jab, we are called to *forgive offenses willingly.*

- It is critical to understand what forgiveness is *not.*
- Forgiveness is not saying, "No problem."
- Forgiveness is not saying, "There's nothing to forgive."
- Forgiveness is not forgetting.
- Forgiveness does not mean that you trust the other person.
- Forgiveness does not necessarily mean that the relationship is restored.
- Forgiveness is not an "event."

In fact, the Christian ideal of *mercy* is based on the Christian understanding of *justice*. The virtue of justice is the act of giving another what he or she is due. Another way to put it is: Justice is paying back what you owe (or getting back what another owes you). Mercy without justice dishonors everyone involved.

It is critical for Christians to begin to understand that we cannot have mercy without justice. In the same way that a person cannot be generous with someone else's property (but only with her own), one cannot be merciful unless she knows how much offering mercy will cost her—and still freely chooses to offer mercy. This is what it is to *forgive offenses willingly.*

*Willingly* is not the same thing as *easily*. First, it means that a person is not forced into choosing forgiveness because of a lack of options. We can probably all think of situations in which we were forced to keep a person in our life, whether a coworker, a family member, or a spouse, and that relationship ultimately festered. Forgiveness was not *willed*; the offense was merely ignored as long as possible.

This is one of the reasons why there can be such brokenness among siblings after their parents pass away. Throughout their lives, the siblings have never willingly forgiven each other; they've merely tolerated the fact that they had to cooperate, or work together, or endure each other's presence. Once the unifying factor (Mom and Dad) is gone, the fact that there has never been real forgiveness is unavoidable.

Real forgiveness has to come from a place of strength. While there are *real* injuries, *real* offenses, and *real* victims, as long as a person sees himself as merely a victim, he will never be able to forgive. Not because he doesn't want to or isn't good enough to offer forgiveness, but because mercy can only be offered by someone who acknowledges his own dignity as well as the weight of the offense to his dignity.

The one who truly forgives has made the decision to tell the truth. She is willing to tell the truth about herself: that while not perfect, she is essentially good. She is worthy of love. She did not deserve to be hurt or used or degraded the way she was. She is also willing to tell the truth about what the offense cost her.

If a person has not discovered this truth—this strength—his act of mercy will often (if not always) be an act of a doormat. Doormats allow people to walk all over them because they lack the strength or ability to do anything else. A Christian who offers forgiveness may absorb another person's act of callousness or injustice, but he does this through an act of the will, aided by God's grace and strength.

Let's consider what is meant by an "act of the will." Traditionally, great thinkers have understood that there are three parts of a human being: intellect (we can think and know), passion (we experience emotions), and will (we can choose). While our emotions are a real part of who we are, many of us make the mistake of basing our decisions on how we are feeling. If forgiveness is an act of the will, a person doesn't have to be disturbed when his or her emotions are still disturbed. Once again, forgiveness does not imply that one's wounds or scars have disappeared. A great forgiver can also be one who continues to suffer much from wounds of the past.

While forgiveness *is* a decision, an act of the will, it is rarely an event. For many of us, forgiveness is a *process*. This implies that there are steps to the process.

First, a person has to realize that he has been hurt. Too many people ignore or dismiss their feelings as unimportant. Remember, if someone has sinned against you, she has violated the dignity of a beloved child of God. You are made for love. It is important that you acknowledge the pain.

Second, since mercy is rooted in justice, one needs to weigh what the other person "owes" him. This step is absolutely crucial. Forgiveness is not an emotion. It is an act of the will (and grace). Therefore, if a person is going to truly choose mercy, he has to use his intellect to know what mercy will cost.

Look at Matthew's Gospel for a picture of this:

> *Then Peter came up and said to him, "Lord, how often shall my brother sin against me, and I forgive him? As many as seven times?" Jesus said to him, "I do not say to you seven times, but seventy times seven.*
>
> *"Therefore the kingdom of heaven may be compared to a king who wished to settle accounts with his servants. When he began the reckoning, one was brought to him who owed him ten thousand talents; and as he could not pay, his lord ordered him to be sold, with his wife and children and all that he had, and payment to be made. So the servant fell on his knees, imploring him, 'Lord, have patience with me, and I will*

> *pay you everything.' And out of pity for him the lord of that servant released him and forgave him the debt." (Matthew 18:21–27)*

In this parable, Jesus makes it absolutely clear that the king knows exactly how much his servant owes him. In fact, the number is given: ten thousand talents! This is more than this man would be able to pay back in multiple lifetimes.

If a person is truly going to forgive, she needs to know how much the other person has "cost" her. I invite each of you (especially if you find yourself plagued by resentment and pain another person has inflicted on you) to try and assess: How much has this person cost you? How have you had to bear the consequences of his choices? How was your childhood robbed by his actions? How have your subsequent relationships been crippled by this person's decisions?

When someone does this, I invite her to do so in the presence of the Blessed Sacrament. It is a safer space, and some of the darker thoughts that can invade one's mind in this exercise can be diffused by the light of Jesus' Eucharistic presence.

Third, after adding up the cost, there is one more step. What happens when the king forgives his servant? Does he have the *emotion* of forgiveness? We don't know. What we do know is that the king, having weighed what the servant has cost him, says, "I release you from your debt." The king is free to make the servant try and repay him (after all, justice reveals that the man owes the king a lot), but he chooses to absorb the cost himself. This doesn't mean, "I trust you." It doesn't mean, "I feel great about you." It doesn't mean, "You and I are best friends now." It simply means, "I will not make you pay me back."

When the Christian is called to *forgive offenses willingly,* he or she is called to make this one decision: "While justice demands that you give me what you owe me, I will not make you pay me back. I release you from your debt."

This is the last thing: Forgiveness is a *process*, not an *event*. You may have to repeat this process many times for the same offense. But each time you do, you will become more and more free, and you will become more and more an image of Jesus Christ himself, who forgives *our* offenses willingly.

---

Father Mike Schmitz is the chaplain for Newman Catholic Campus Ministry at the University of Minnesota Duluth.

*"I urge that supplications, prayers, intercessions, and thanksgivings be made for all men."*

*1 TIMOTHY 2:1*

14

# PRAY FOR THE LIVING AND THE DEAD

**PRAYER IS A BY-PRODUCT** of hope. Hope is something you can't buy but is freely given if you ask. Hope is the one thing people cannot live without. Hope, like mercy, is beautiful.

# EMPATHETIC MERCY

*JOHN MICHAEL TALBOT*

We pray for others from the "bowels of mercy." In every major office of the Liturgy of the Hours, and in the Mass, we include intercessions.

All the Greek words indicate that *mercy* means both "sympathy" and an "empathy" that is deeply compassionate. Having sympathy means to be compassionate from the outside in. But empathy is something far more. Having empathy means to be compassionate from the inside out. It means to get right inside the person we care about and understand him or her from inside out. It is "from the bowels."

But sometimes we do not even understand ourselves, much less others (see Romans 7:15). In his *Confessions,* St. Augustine says, "You were within me, but I was outside."[20]

Here's the good news. God knows us better than we know ourselves because he is closer to us than we are to ourselves. No one knows a person but the spirit of that person (see 1 Corinthians 2:10), and sometimes we only really find ourselves when we lose ourselves completely for Jesus (see Matthew 16:24–25).

When we pray for mercy, we ask God to forgive and strengthen us in ways beyond what we can know or understand. He knows us better than we know ourselves, and he loves us more than we love ourselves. Mercy means trusting completely in that divine yet most human reality.

There are many kinds of prayer, including petition and intercession. Not all prayer is petition and intercession, but all petition and intercession in Christ is prayer.

When we pray for others, we focus our attention on their needs; we allow ourselves to really sympathize and empathize with them as much as we are able with the assistance of the Holy Spirit, and we experience a communion in Christ with them that transcends images or words and is as constant as every breath we take. We simply become an intercession and petition for others as we become more and more fully in communion in Christ.

Traditionally we understand *petition*, or biblical supplication, as asking for something, and *intercession* as actually standing *with* someone—or even in his or her place—through the intercession of Jesus Christ. This is radical stuff!

In the New Testament the Greek word for *petition* and *intercession* is similar. It is used of Jesus, who is the primary intercessor (see Hebrews 7:25). The prophet Isaiah provides the classical Christian understanding of intercession in Jesus.

> *Surely he has borne our griefs and carried our sorrows; yet we esteemed him stricken, struck down by God, and afflicted. But he was wounded for our transgressions, he was bruised for our iniquities; upon him was the chastisement*

> *that made us whole, and with his stripes we are healed. All we like sheep have gone astray; we have turned every one to his own ay; and the Lord has laid on him the iniquity of us all. (Isaiah 53:4–6)*

Is this a mean and angry God punishing his own Son? I think not. Jesus says it is all about love. He says, "Greater love has no man than this, that a man lay down his life for his friends. You are my friends. . ." (John 15:13–14).

This is the amazing love of Jesus Christ. This is real intercession—that God loves us so much that he gave his life for us personally. From eternity God knows every joy and sorrow, every tragedy and triumph, every laughter and every tear. It is personal, intimate, and life changing!

And he gives this gift to you and me personally. Imagine that the likes of you and me can actually share in this gift of interceding for everyone alive and dead in this amazing love of Jesus Christ. We are not worthy. We are just sinners saved by grace. But we actually get to embark on this greatest of ministries, to intercede in Christ for everyone everywhere. It is too big for us, but not too big for Jesus. All things really are possible with God!

Scripture is filled with asking for and offering prayers for those alive, and even raising the dead with those prayers. But what about praying for the dead? Saul was condemned for communicating with the dead via the witch at Endor (see 1 Samuel 28:8), and Jesus teaches in the Parable of the Rich Man and Lazarus that there is no need to communicate with the dead if someone won't first listen to God, and those he sent in history (see Luke16:19–31).

But this is not the same as praying for the departed and asking departed saints to pray for us. This was already a clear part of Judaism in the time of Christ (see 2 Maccabees 12:43–46), and it was the practice of the first Christians. Paul speaks of the curious practice of baptism for the dead in 1 Corinthians 15:29. We know that the catacombs in Rome, which give a clear window into the worship and beliefs of the earliest Christians, contain prayers for the dead and prayers asking for the intercession of the saintly dead in Christ. The Scriptures mention this too (see Revelation 5:8).

The basic belief is that nothing, neither life nor death, can separate us from the love of Christ (see Romans 8:35). Our "communion," or "common union," as a united people in that love of Christ cannot be broken even in death. Love defies the limitations of time and space.

Praying for the faithful departed is an expression of great love in Christ. Asking for the prayers of those who were most saintly, and recognized as such by the Church, is an act of humility in the communion of the saints that only Jesus fully offers. It is a beautiful expression of the communion of the saints. But we must be careful not to engage in communication with the dead that could open us up to lying spirits who claim to be saints but are not. Many have been deceived by evil spirits appearing as angels of light, who are really angels of darkness (see 2 Corinthians 11:11–14).

Finally, we must pray with faith. Jesus says that if we do not believe that what we ask for will happen, it won't (see Mark 11:22–24). But we must also forgive, and be humble. We must "expect a miracle," or we won't see any. And we must "accept" the kind of miracle God gives, or we will sin through presumption. Many fail in both aspects of this saying, and thus their prayers are ineffectual.

Faith is the substance, essence, or personification of things hoped for, of things we don't yet see (see Hebrews 11:1). We must personify in the now the things we only hope for in the future. Pray with such faith and you will see miracles for others, and for yourself as well.

We have the wonderful privilege to be able to pray with petition and the intercessory power of Jesus Christ for those most in need of his mercy—both those who are alive and those who are departed. This is more than just rattling off prayers with a perfunctory "Lord, hear our prayer" at the end. This is deep, gut-wrenching, love-pervaded prayer. It's prayer on your knees or prostrate before God. Liturgical space and time might not accommodate this externally, but it must be our inner attitude. There is always a sense of victory in these prayers. Jesus has died, risen, and ascended, and he has given us his Spirit to pray for all those most in need of his mercy with the confidence of faith.

---

John Michael Talbot is a bestselling author and pioneering recording artist.

# INFINITE MERCY

*MSGR. CHARLES POPE*

What is the value of one prayer? I suspect it is far greater than any of us imagine. Prayer changes things, sometimes in obvious ways, more often in subtle and even paradoxical ways. But prayer is surely important, even when we don't experience its immediate effects. Perhaps this is why Jesus taught us to pray always and never to lose heart (see Luke 18:1). St. Paul echoed this with the simple exhortation "Pray constantly" (1 Thessalonians 5:17). St. James also warned, "You do not have, because you do not ask" (James 4:2).

Perhaps one of the greatest joys of heaven will be seeing how much of a difference our prayers made, even the distracted and perfunctory ones. Perhaps our simple utterance at the end of a decade of the Rosary to "save us from the fires of hell and lead all souls to heaven" will reach the heart of one lost soul, prompting him to answer the gentle call of God to return. Imagine if someday in heaven that very sinner comes up to you and says, "Though we never met, your prayer reached me and God applied his power to me." Imagine the joy of many such meetings in heaven. Imagine, too, whom *you* will joyfully thank for their prayers, people you know and some you never met. But they prayed, and the power of their prayers reached you.

So to pray for the living is a great and wondrous spiritual work of mercy; its value is beyond gold or pearls. Yes, what is the value of one prayer? "The prayer of a righteous man has great power in its effects" (James 5:16). Prayer can avert war, bring healing, cause conversion, bestow peace and serenity, and call down mercy—sweet, necessary, and beautiful mercy. Prayer is inestimable; its value can never be told.

Praying for the dead, however, is a spiritual work of mercy that has suffered in recent decades. Too many Catholics today "miss a step" when loved ones die. There are often immediate declarations that the deceased are "in heaven" or are "in a better place." But Scripture doesn't say that we go right to heaven when we die. No, indeed, there is a brief stopover at the judgment seat of Christ.

The Letter to the Hebrews says, "It is appointed for men to die once, and after that comes judgment" (Hebrews 9:27). And St. Paul writes, "For we must all appear before the judgment seat of Christ, so that each one may receive good or evil, according to what he has done in the body" (2 Corinthians 5:10).

So our deceased loved ones go to the judgment seat of Christ. And *that* is worth praying about!

But what is the judgment in question for those who lived faithful lives? In such cases, the judgment is not merely about the ultimate destination of heaven or hell. The judgment in question would seem to be "Is my work in you complete?"

Indeed, the Lord has made all of us a promise: "You, therefore, must be perfect, as your heavenly Father is perfect" (Matthew 5:48). Such a beautiful promise! And yet most of us know that we are not in such a state now; if we were to die today it is clear that much work would still be required. And thus when we send our faithful loved ones to judgment, though we send them with hope, we are aware that finishing work may be necessary. Purgation and purification are necessary before entering heaven, of which Scripture says, "Nothing unclean shall enter it" (Revelation 21:27).

Again, this is worth praying about. It is a great work of mercy we can extend to our deceased loved ones, to remember them with love and to pray, in the words of St. Paul, "[May God] who has begun a good work in you...bring it to completion" (Philippians 1:6). Pray often for the souls in purgatory. Surely there are joys there for them, knowing that they are on their way to heaven. But surely, too, there are sufferings that purgation must cause. St. Paul says of purgatory:

> *Each man's work will become manifest, for the Day will disclose it, because it will be revealed with fire, and the fire will test what sort of work each one has done. If the work which any man has built on the foundation survives, he will receive a reward. If any man's work is burned up, he will suffer loss, though he himself will be saved, but only as through fire. (1 Corinthians 3:13–15)*

Yes, there is fire, but thank God it is a healing fire. There are tears, too, for Scripture says (regarding the dead) that Jesus "will wipe away every tear from their eyes" (Revelations 21:4).

How consoling and merciful our prayers must seem to our beloved who have died! How prayers must seem like a gentle wind that speeds them along, onward and upward toward heaven!

Praying for the dead, then, is the last and greatest spiritual work of mercy. For by the grace of it, and through its help, souls attain the glory God has prepared for them from the foundation of the world.

---

Msgr. Charles Pope is the pastor of Holy Comforter-St. Cyprian, a parish community in Washington, D.C.

# CONCLUSION: BEYOND GRUMBLING

*DR. SCOTT HAHN*

Everybody felt it: a moment of eerie silence, a low rumble and then the ground began to shake. Buildings swayed and buckled, then collapsed like houses of cards. Less than four minutes later, over thirty thousand were dead from a magnitude 8.2 earthquake that rocked and nearly flattened Armenia in 1989.

In the muddled chaos a distressed father bolted through the winding streets leading to the school where his son had gone earlier that morning. The man couldn't stop thinking about the promise he'd given his son many times: "No matter what happens, Armand, I'll always be there."

He reached the site where the school had been, but saw only a pile of rubble. He just stood there at first, fighting back tears, then took off, stumbling over debris, toward the east corner where he knew his son's classroom had been.

With nothing but his bare hands, he started to dig. He was desperately pulling up bricks and pieces of wall-plaster, while others stood by watching in forlorn disbelief. He heard someone growl, "Forget it, mister. They're all dead."

He looked up, flustered, and replied, "You can grumble, or you can help me lift these bricks." Only a few pitched in, and most of them gave up once their muscles began to ache. But the man couldn't stop thinking about his son.

He kept digging and digging—for hours. . . .twelve hours. . . . eighteen hours. . .twenty-four hours. . .thirty-six hours. . . Finally, into the thirty-eighth hour, he heard a muffled groan from under a piece of wallboard.

He seized the board, pulled it back, and cried, "ARMAND!" From the darkness came a slight, shaking voice calling, "Papa. . .!"

Other weak voices began calling out, as the young survivors stirred beneath the still-uncleared rubble. Gasps and shouts of bewildered relief came from the few onlookers and parents who remained. They found fourteen of the thirty-three students still alive.

When Armand finally emerged, he tried to help dig until all his surviving classmates were out. Everybody standing there heard him as he turned to his friends and said, "See, I told you my father wouldn't forget us."

That's the kind faith we need, because that's the kind of Father we have.

Our Heavenly Father has been watching over us throughout all of history, saving us from destruction over and over again. He longs to convince us of his passionate love for each one of us, that relentless mercy which calls—and enables—us to share his own divine life, that fiery outpouring of love by which the Father eternally begets the Son in the Holy Spirit. Only an infinite, raging love such as appears among the Blessed Trinity can explain the mysteries of human sin and salvation.

Let's face it, we humans really don't want God to love us *that* much. It's simply too demanding. Obedience is one thing, but this sort of love calls for more than keeping commandments. It calls for nothing less than total self-donation. That might not be a difficult job for the three infinite Persons of the Trinity, but for creatures like us, such love is a summons to martyrdom. This invisible love requires much more suffering and self-denial than simply giving up chocolate for Lent. It demands nothing less than a constant dying to self.

We desperately need God's mercy and grace. We'd like to think there's a simpler solution—more education, laws, technology, or money. That's almost like prescribing aspirin for AIDS! Sin's infection is too deep and too deadly. But we shouldn't despair or get depressed. Our Father knows what we need better than we do. "Once we were also ruled by the selfish desires of our bodies and minds. We had made God angry, and we were going to be punished. But God was merciful! We were dead because of our sins, but God loved us so much that he made us alive with Christ" (Ephesians 2:3–4, CEV).

Here on earth the Church is a field full of both wheat and weeds, as Jesus himself taught in the parables of the kingdom of heaven (see Matthew 13:24–30, 36–43). But she is really and truly the heavenly kingdom even here on earth. "The Church [is]. . . at once holy and always in need of purification" (*CCC,* 827). She embraces saints and sinners. Sometimes we see only the sinners.

Through Scripture we must train ourselves to attain a sacramental vision of the Church. Don't ever let the mixed bag that is the Church on earth cause you to leave her or stay out of her. When you allow scandal to make you leave the Church or stay out of the Church, you are not only depriving yourself of the spiritual food of the sacraments, you are spurning Christ's Bride.

St. Cyprian once said, "You cannot have God as your Father without the Church as your Mother." Perhaps John would paraphrase this, "If you will not have the Bride, then cut yourself off from the Bridegroom."

Sinners are in the Church, but they do not embody the Church. For them the Church is a hospital for healing—so they can be made into saints. The sacraments, the liturgy, and especially the saints embody the Church's true essence. The saints embody John's vision of what the Church is and what her members are supposed to be.

The crisis of the Church is not reducible to the lack of good catechists, liturgies, theologians, and so forth. It's a crisis of saints. But it's a crisis that our Father can be trusted to handle, especially if we allow him to keep his promises to us. "I am sure that he who began a good work in you will bring it to completion at the day of Jesus Christ" (Philippians 1:6). So with Pope John Paul II, I urge you, "Make yourselves saints, and do so quickly!"

---

Dr. Scott Hahn is a popular speaker, teacher, and author.

# NOTES

# ENDNOTES

1 *The Merchant of Venice*, Act IV, Scene I, Line 163.

2 Interview, September 30, 2013.

3 Ibid.

4 Pope John Paul II, "What Is Divine Mercy?" The Divine Mercy, http://www.thedivinemercy.org/message/johnpaul/.

5 Saint Maria Faustina Kowalska, *Diary of Saint Maria Faustina Kowalska: Divine Mercy in My Soul* (Stockbridge, MA: Marian Press, 1981), entry 723.

6 Pope Francis, "Misericordiae Vultus: Bull of Indiction of the Extraordinary Jubilee of Mercy," April 11, 2015, paragraph 2.

7 Ibid., 9.

8 Ibid., 15.

9 Dr. Robert Stackpole, STD, "Part 10: The Corporal Works of Mercy," The Divine Mercy, September 7, 2009, http://www.thedivinemercy.org/library/article.php?NID=3479.

10 Kowalska, *Diary of Saint Maria Faustina Kowalska*, 1777.

11 Ibid., 1541.

12 Ibid., 811.

13 "Eucharistic Apostles of the Divine Mercy," The Divine Mercy, http://www.thedivinemercy.org/eadm/praying.php.

14 Stackpole, "Part 10: The Corporal Works of Mercy."

15 John Paul II, *Memory and Identity*, 55.

16 Pope Paul VI, *Evangelii Nuntiandi*, 14. 1975

17 Joseph Cardinal Ratzinger, *Gospel Catechesis Catechism* (San Francisco: Ignatius Press, 1997) p. 44.

18 http://blog.adw.org/2015/05/counsel-the-doubtful-a-meditation-on-the-third-spiritual-work-of-mercy/

19 John Paul II, *Redemptoris Missio*, 33.

20 *The Confessions of St. Augustine*, Book X, 27.

# NOTES

# NOTES

# NOTES

# NOTES

# THE DYNAMIC CATHOLIC INSTITUTE

## [MISSION]

To re-energize the Catholic Church in America by developing world-class resources that inspire people to rediscover the genius of Catholicism.

## [VISION]

To be the innovative leader in the New Evangelization helping Catholics and their parishes become the-best-version-of-themselves

**Join us in re-energizing the Catholic Church.**
***Become a Dynamic Catholic Ambassador today!***